"This is a beautiful page-turner of a book, a must-read for all who engage in teaching the Christian faith. Whether you are in the church or the classroom, just embarking upon your calling or have been teaching for decades, Neder's powerful, grace-bathed theological reflections on teaching the Christian faith will impact why and how you do what you do."

—**Kristen Deede Johnson,**
Western Theological Seminary

"Here is a volume of warmth and wisdom on teaching theology. Drawing heavily on the insight of figures like Barth, Bonhoeffer, and Kierkegaard, Neder points us to lived theology that is personal and vibrant, honest and faithful. Encouragements—and warnings—bounce off the pages as Neder provides tried and tested counsel on good teaching and healthy classroom practices, all done with and before the triune God: we have much to learn from him!"

—**Kelly M. Kapic,** Covenant College;
author of *A Little Book for New Theologians*

"The person you meet in this book is a deeply serious, self-critical Christian gentleman, who is passionately discipled to the person and work of Jesus Christ and who yearns for the discipline of theology to be taught compassionately, intelligently, and engagingly. If Neder were to write a comprehensive account of Christian theology, I would be as eager to read it as I once was to read Karl Barth's *Church Dogmatics*."

—**Frederick Dale Bruner**,
Union Theological Seminary, Philippines,
and Whitworth University (emeritus)

"What does it mean to be 'in Christ'? Neder wonders what it means to *teach* 'in Christ.' For those of us in academia or pastoring a congregation, this comes as both a challenge and a gift. Neder joins Barth's ever-present call to 'theological existence' in which not just the content but the praxis of our teaching is changed by the person of Christ. Prayer, personal integration, humility, and even publishing are discussed in this light (with the help of World Cup and Radiohead analogies). As Neder says, 'Teaching Christianity is an act of love.' So is this book."

—**Julie Canlis**, Whitworth University

THEOLOGY

AS A

WAY OF LIFE

THEOLOGY

AS A

WAY OF LIFE

ON TEACHING AND LEARNING

THE CHRISTIAN FAITH

ADAM NEDER

Baker Academic

a division of Baker Publishing Group

Grand Rapids, Michigan

© 2019 by Adam Neder

Published by Baker Academic
a division of Baker Publishing Group
PO Box 6287, Grand Rapids, MI 49516-6287
www.bakeracademic.com

Printed in the United States of America

Library of Congress Cataloging-in-Publication Data
Names: Neder, Adam, author.
Title: Theology as a way of life : on teaching and learning the Christian
    faith / Adam Neder.
Description: Grand Rapids, MI : Baker Academic a division of Baker
    Publishing Group, [2019] | Includes bibliographical references and index.
Identifiers: LCCN 2019006258 | ISBN 9780801098789 (pbk.)
Subjects: LCSH: Theology—Study and teaching.
Classification: LCC BV4020 .N38 2019 | DDC 230.071—dc23
LC record available at https://lccn.loc.gov/2019006258

978-1-5409-6245-4 (casebound)

Scripture quotations are from the New Revised Standard Version of the Bible, copyright © 1989 National
Council of the Churches of Christ in the United States
of America. Used by permission. All rights reserved.

19 20 21 22 23 24 25   7 6 5 4 3 2 1

For Reginald McLelland
and Bruce McCormack

CONTENTS

Abbreviations xi

Introduction 1

1. Identity 15

2. Knowledge 37

3. Ethos 61

4. Danger 85

5. Conversation 113

Bibliography 147

Index 155

ABBREVIATIONS

CD	*Church Dogmatics*
DBWE	*Dietrich Bonhoeffer Works*
ET	*Evangelical Theology: An Introduction*
KJN	*Kierkegaard's Journals and Notebooks*
rev.	revised translation

INTRODUCTION

This book began as a paper for the annual Karl Barth conference at Princeton Theological Seminary in 2012. The theme of the conference was Barth's book *Evangelical Theology*, which contains the lectures he gave during his only visit to the United States.[1] As I was thinking about what I might say, I began to notice that Barth's reflections on the task of writing Christian theology could be slightly adjusted to illuminate the task of teaching Christian theology.[2] Having spent the previous decade struggling to formulate a compelling theological and spiritual understanding of teaching, this came as a welcome relief. As a young professor I knew I needed guidance, but my

1. Karl Barth, *Evangelical Theology: An Introduction*, trans. Grover Foley (Grand Rapids: Eerdmans, 1963).

2. The paper was published as "'The Sun Behind the Clouds': Some Barthian Thoughts about Teaching Christian Theology," in *Karl Barth and the Making of "Evangelical Theology": A Fifty-Year Perspective*, ed. Clifford B. Anderson and Bruce L. McCormack (Grand Rapids: Eerdmans, 2015), 222–35.

search for books that could help me think seriously
about teaching Christian theology proved far more
difficult than I had imagined, which seemed strange
to me. When so much theological education happens in classrooms, why haven't theologians written
persuasively about what goes on there? Shouldn't we
have numerous good books about teaching theology?
We have good books about education and teaching in
general, about Christian liberal arts education, and
about the history of theological education, but none
written by a contemporary theologian about the art of
teaching Christian theology. Yet without a compelling
theological vision of what it means to teach Christian
theology well, and without a clear awareness of its
unique challenges and temptations, our instruction
will be out of joint with the subject matter, and valuable opportunities will be wasted.

Eventually I decided that if no one else was going
to write the book, then I would. Not because I think I
am an especially good teacher. Anyone who claims to
have mastered the art of teaching Christianity is a fool.
No one possesses the necessary knowledge, wisdom,
eloquence, or imagination. Only the self-deceived arrive at the end of a semester thinking a course went as
well as it could have gone. Anyone who doesn't find

it strange that he or she should be the one to stand in front of a group of people and talk about God is either deluded or hasn't thought very deeply about what is happening. No one has the power to make God present. Everyone persuades people to believe things that are not true. Every teacher's life somehow contradicts the subject matter. At some point, every teacher leads students away from God.

I didn't write this book because I think I am an exception to any of this. Whatever authority I possess is merely the result of trying to think carefully about the difference Jesus Christ makes for theological education. If he is truly God and truly human, if he reveals God to us and us to ourselves, if "through him God was pleased to reconcile to himself all things" (Col. 1:20), then how should that influence the way we think about teaching the Christian faith? How do we develop a specifically Christian approach to teaching Christian theology? This book is the result of years of struggling with this question, however unsatisfactorily.

Please don't think this is false humility. I have been a professor at Whitworth University for the past sixteen years. Most of my students think I am a good teacher. I know that because they tell me so and because they write sweet things in their course evaluations. But with every year that passes I become more acutely aware of my weaknesses, more in touch with the ways I fail them. My guess is that many teachers feel this way. We know we're not up to the challenge, and so we wonder, *Okay, well now what?* We've been given an impossible task. We want students to know God—not merely to know about God, but to know God personally. We want them to engage with Scripture, doctrine, art, history, philosophy, and plenty of other things, but knowledge of those things is not our ultimate goal—or at least it shouldn't be. In the midst of all this, we hope our classrooms become places where students encounter the living God—places where they become contemporaneous with Christ, to use Søren Kierkegaard's way of speaking. Theology is not for the sake of theology but for the sake of life. As Kierkegaard put it, "The truth, if it is there, is a being, a *life*"—indeed, the truth is known only "when it becomes a life in me."[3] The goal of theological study is not merely to understand but "to exist in what one understands," and that kind of knowledge is not something teachers can engineer in their

3. Søren Kierkegaard, *Practice in Christianity*, ed. and trans. Howard V. Hong and Edna H. Hong (Princeton: Princeton University Press, 1991), 206.

students, nor can students realize it on their own.[4] It depends ultimately on God himself.[5] But if teachers are incapable of accomplishing our most basic task, of achieving our most important goal, shouldn't that shape the way we teach? And if so, how?

Much recent thinking conceives Christian education as largely a process of socialization in which students are habituated into the Christian life through repetitive practices that lead to virtue. The approach is broadly Augustinian and has numerous strengths. James K. A. Smith is its most influential proponent.[6] Smith argues that most Christian education suffers from a faulty anthropology that sees human beings as essentially thinking creatures whose minds need to be filled with information that adds up to a Christian worldview. Against this view, Smith argues that human beings are "oriented primarily by desire; by what we love,"

4. Søren Kierkegaard, *Concluding Unscientific Postscript to* Philosophical Fragments, ed. and trans. Howard V. Hong and Edna H. Hong (Princeton: Princeton University Press, 1992), 274.

5. Our language is inadequate. Since God is not male, I am sympathetic to the claim that referring to God with masculine pronouns can be misleading. That is a valid concern. However, I have not been persuaded that the available alternatives are less misleading.

6. See James K. A. Smith, *Desiring the Kingdom: Worship, Worldview, and Cultural Formation* (Grand Rapids: Baker Academic, 2009), and *You Are What You Love: The Spiritual Power of Habit* (Grand Rapids: Brazos, 2016).

and therefore that Christian education is primarily about formation rather than information.[7] Christian education aims to reeducate desire through the cultivation of habit-forming practices that orient students' precognitive assumptions about the world toward the kingdom of God.

There is much to agree with and appreciate in Smith's work, and our goals overlap significantly, but readers familiar with Smith's books will find themselves in a different atmosphere here. The core theological claim of this book is that Jesus Christ establishes the truth of human identity in his life, death, and resurrection. We are who we are because Jesus is who he is. That is an objective fact that is true about everyone—a reality acknowledged and enacted by individuals as the Holy Spirit awakens and empowers them to discover and embrace their lives in Christ, to become who they already are in him. I introduce this position in the first chapter, and the rest of the book unfolds from there. Smith's thesis that we are shaped by our habitual "liturgies" seems clearly correct to me, and it is true that in a certain sense we are what we love. But in the soil of Smith's more traditional anthropology, becoming

7. Smith, *Desiring the Kingdom*, 25.

who we are means something different than it does to someone operating with the kind of christological anthropology that animates my work, and this leads to important differences in our respective approaches. I don't intend this as a criticism, and I don't think Smith will receive it as one, since we develop our anthropologies from such obviously different starting points. We need more people engaged in the kind of work Smith is doing, and I certainly have no desire to criticize him. In fact, I think our approaches mutually enrich each other's in helpful ways.

Readers will quickly recognize how indebted I am to the work of Søren Kierkegaard, Karl Barth, and Dietrich Bonhoeffer. But I would like to be clear from the outset that this book is not about those great thinkers. While they have taught me more than anyone else about teaching theology, and while I draw on them extensively throughout the book, my primary goal is not to describe their thought. Instead, I am trying to think along with them—to let what I have learned from them inform my own reflections about teaching Christian theology. And to readers suspicious of these writers, I ask for patience and a willingness to suspend judgment. Good conversations do not require agreement on first principles, and readers with different theological commitments, especially from those in the first chapter, may nevertheless find themselves sympathetic to much of what they encounter here.

It is important to understand that this book is not a collection of practical tips about how to create a syllabus, structure a class, write an exam, grade a paper, or the like. Every teacher needs to know how to do these things, but we already have plenty of good books on these subjects. As far as practical suggestions, the concluding chapter on conversation offers the most concrete guidance. In fact, this is not even a book about what to teach or how to teach it. Whatever one's ecclesial tradition, I assume that everyone who teaches Christian theology agrees that it involves the communication of the content, grammar, history, and significance of Christian doctrine. Beyond that, every teacher will have his or her own reasons for what material to include and what style to adopt, and these will be influenced by a number of factors, including one's social and institutional location, the specific needs of one's students, and one's own knowledge, capacities, and theological commitments. Teaching theology is an art, and art cannot be standardized.

While I teach undergraduate and graduate classes in historical and systematic theology at a Christian university, the framework offered here is broad enough to include anyone who teaches the Christian faith in any context, including and especially in local congregations. I hope the book will be as useful to pastors, Christian educators, and informal study group leaders as it will be to university and seminary professors. While I rarely draw connections to congregational ministry, these connections are always just beneath the surface and not difficult to imagine. And with only slight adjustments, most of what I say about teaching Christian theology applies to teaching any theological discipline, whether in formal or informal contexts. The future of teaching Christian theology in this country is obviously not in universities. Most universities have long since ceased to offer classes in Christian doctrine taught by Christian theologians in distinctly Christian ways. The number of universities in America where it is possible to take classes in Christian theology from a professor who openly confesses belief in the truth of God's self-revelation in Christ, and who attempts to teach in a way that is faithful to that reality, is smaller than perhaps many Christians realize.

The lack of such institutions largely explains why so many excellent theologians have no prospect of a tenure-track university position. Anecdotally, when the

Whitworth theology department opens a search for a new faculty position, we receive hundreds of applications from scholars around the world, most of whom are qualified, and many of whom would do well here, but we hire only one of them, and the job market remains flooded. Meanwhile, the church sinks deeper into its educational crisis, one where most Christians have trouble articulating even the most basic Christian doctrines, and where they receive very little if any training to think creatively about the difference Christian theology makes for navigating ordinary life. And this at a time when Christians in the Western world are encountering more persuasive counter-narratives about the meaning of human existence than they have for a very long time.

I suppose I should also say something about the style of this book. By speaking informally and addressing teachers personally, I have broken with some of the standard conventions of academic theological writing. But then why would one want to adhere to them anyway? It's hard to imagine anyone outside our discipline wanting to write like we write. Teaching theology is a serious matter, and I am trying to make a serious argument, but adopting a more abstract, technical, and impersonal tone of voice, or writing in more conventional academic prose, wouldn't make what I say any more true or persuasive. It would only make it boring.

A number of friends—too many to list—have read previous drafts of this book and offered valuable suggestions. They know who they are, and I hope they know how much I appreciate their help. I am especially grateful to my editor, David Nelson, who attended the conference in Princeton and encouraged me to write this book. In my position as the Bruner-Welch Professor of Theology at Whitworth, I receive unusually generous support, and I am thankful for that too.

Before moving on, I'd like to say a word about the two people to whom this book is dedicated. In the fall semester of my sophomore year at Covenant College, I took a class in philosophical theology from Reginald McLelland, who introduced me to a way of thinking about the Christian faith that was unlike anything I had previously encountered. The class changed the whole course of my life. One afternoon late in the semester, I remember thinking, *If I somehow manage to do for two or three people what Dr. McLelland has done for me, that would be a good career. I'd take that.* That was twenty-six years ago, and my gratitude and affection for him have only increased since. I often wonder about this.

Why do we love our best theology teachers so much? Why are we so thankful for them? Why do we have such strong loyalty, respect, and affection for people like St. Augustine, C. S. Lewis, and Reg McLelland? It must be at least partially because we've had to suffer under so many bad teachers—people whose lectures, sermons, essays, and books confuse us more than they enlighten us, teachers with a perverse knack for making the Christian faith seem tedious and pointless. I suspect many readers of this book know what it feels like to care deeply about being a Christian—to know you're not very good at it and to long for someone to take you by the hand and show you a better way. You understand what it's like to be almost desperate for insight. But then your teachers teach . . . and nothing happens. Or worse than nothing—you feel more confused and discouraged than you did before they started teaching. But if you somehow manage to find a teacher who casts light rather than darkness, someone who ushers you into "the strange new world within the Bible"[8] and the deep mysteries of the Christian faith, someone who helps you see yourself and everything else in the light

8. This well-known phrase is a wonderful mistranslation of the title of Karl Barth's 1917 essay "The New World in the Bible," which can be found in *The Word of God and Theology*, trans. Amy Marga (London: T&T Clark, 2011), 15–30.

of Christ, you know that few things in life are better than a good teacher. And being McLelland's student has certainly been one of the best parts of my life.

When I arrived in Princeton in the summer of 1996, I had never heard of Bruce McCormack. By the time I left in 2003, I owed more to him professionally than to anyone else. Bruce's clarity of thought and expression, his disciplined and expansive theological imagination, and his prodigious Barth scholarship are exemplary in the field. But more than anything else, Bruce showed me that good teachers give their students freedom. They offer students space to make up their own minds, to find their own ways forward. Aware of their fallibility, the limitations of their perspective, and the difference between their knowledge of God and God's knowledge of himself, good teachers don't seek to reproduce themselves in students. Of course they want to be persuasive, and Bruce certainly is, but they never coerce students or require them to conform to their views. Their goal is not to create loyal soldiers who repeat and defend the master, but to train students to listen to God's Word, discover their own voices, and respond to Jesus Christ's call in their own ways. Of all the things that Bruce has taught me about teaching Christian theology, I appreciate that the most.

1

IDENTITY

Anthropology is the soul of pedagogy. Who we think our students are animates how we teach them. However conscious or unconscious, clear or ambiguous, coherent or incoherent, our working anthropology shapes our pedagogical goals and practices. As we seek to understand particular students, we draw on an understanding of human beings in general. This is no less true for teachers who reject the idea of human nature as such, since that too is rooted in a view of what human beings are. And yet at first glance, the question of what makes human beings human appears unanswerable. No two people are exactly alike. Each of us is distinguished by our differences, those collective differences are boundless, and it's impossible to account for them all. The question of what unites us amid our differences runs the risk of generating answers too narrow to include everyone—an error with a long history of calamitous consequences. Furthermore, our rapidly expanding knowledge resists summary. From neuroscience to literature, psychology to economics, genetics to political science, we are awash with illuminating lenses through which to understand people. No single discipline— much less a single individual—is capable of synthesizing all the insights relevant to the construction of a comprehensive theory of the human person. There is always more to learn. And given our numerous limitations and biases, developing a broadly compelling theory seems impossible anyway. Thus teachers face an apparent dilemma: either we conclude that an adequate view of human nature cannot be constructed, or we prioritize a particular disciplinary perspective, even when that perspective cannot accommodate important or competing evidence. Neither option looks promising.

Karl Barth offers a revolutionary Christian response to this dilemma, one that informs more or less everything I say about teaching in this book. His basic thesis is that Jesus Christ is "the one Archimedean point given to us beyond humanity, and therefore the one possibility of discovering" what it means to be truly human.[1] In other words, Jesus Christ is the key that unlocks the mystery of human nature. He is the true human being. In him we discover not only who God is but also who we are. As God "discloses himself to us, he also discloses us to ourselves."[2] This insight does not replace or compete with what we learn about humanity from other disciplines; Barth counsels us to welcome the contributions made by the various disciplines to our understanding of human life. Instead, his christological anthropology contextualizes that knowledge within a fundamental relationship. Whatever else turns out to be true about us, the relationship secured between God and humanity in Christ is the basic presupposition of human life. Human nature has no "independent signification" apart from this relationship.[3]

The church has always struggled to fully grasp this point. For all its strengths, the long history of Christian

1. CD 3.2:132. See my book *Participation in Christ: An Entry into Karl Barth's "Church Dogmatics"* (Louisville: Westminster John Knox, 2009), 29–39.

2. CD 4.2:300.

3. CD 2.2:8. See also Søren Kierkegaard's claim that it is "the God-relationship that makes a human being into a human being" (*The Sickness unto Death*, ed. and trans. Howard V. Hong and Edna H. Hong [Princeton: Princeton University Press, 1980], 79).

reflection on human nature is marked by a speculative tendency to look away from its center in Christ. While the concept of the image of God has dominated Christian reflection about what it means to be human, the numerous interpretations given to that phrase have rarely been consistently governed by the New Testament's identification of Jesus Christ as himself the image of God, and they have often gone far beyond anything suggested in the Old Testament passages that use the phrase.[4] Against this tendency, an anthropology rooted in Christ's person and work offers resources for conceiving of the image of God—and the essential truth of humanity in general—not as a particular faculty, attribute, or set of attributes intrinsic to each individual person, but rather as a living relationship established by God in Christ, which includes everyone and into which everyone is called. Since that is a compressed and rather cryptic way of expressing this crucial point, I will now explain what I mean.

The Reality of Reconciliation

The New Testament describes the relationship God establishes with the world in Christ using a wealth of

4. See Gen. 1:26–27; 5:1; 9:6; 2 Cor. 4:4; Col. 1:15; Heb. 1:3.

images and metaphors, among the most important of which is reconciliation (Greek *katallage*). While the word and related terms appear infrequently in the New Testament, their significance is nevertheless unmistakable. For example, Paul uses reconciliation language five times in 2 Corinthians 5:18–21—a passage that includes his magisterial assertion that "in Christ God was reconciling the world to himself" (v. 19). The word indicates the setting right of a relationship. God's reconciliation of the world to himself in Christ is his decisive intervention against everything that impedes this relationship. Commenting on this verse, Barth writes that in Christ "the weakness and godlessness and sin and enmity of the world are shown to be a lie and objectively removed once and for all. And there, too, in Christ, the peace of the world with God, the turning of humanity to him, its friendship with God, is shown to be the truth and objectively confirmed once and for all."[5]

But as one reflects on claims such as this, an important question begins to emerge. Is it true to say that the reconciliation Jesus Christ accomplished in his life, death, and resurrection is an "objective" reality? Did

5. CD 4.1:76.

he really establish peace between God and humanity?
Is that a fact that includes everyone—something that
is true about each and every one of our students? Or
did Jesus Christ make it only *possible* for people to be
reconciled to God? Did he open a way to reconciliation that becomes real only when people respond to
it appropriately? In other words, does our response
make reconciliation a reality, or does the reality of reconciliation call forth our response? Our answers to
these questions have far-reaching consequences, both
for how we understand what it means to be human
and for how we teach Christian theology.

Consider the three most important New Testament
passages that bear upon this issue. As you read them,
pay attention to whether they move from the possibility of right response to the reality of reconciliation,
or from the reality of reconciliation to the possibility
of right response.

Romans 5:6–11

> For while we were still weak, at the right time Christ
> died for the ungodly. Indeed, rarely will anyone die
> for a righteous person—though perhaps for a good
> person someone might actually dare to die. But God

proves his love for us in that while we still were sinners Christ died for us. Much more surely then, now that we have been justified by his blood, will we be saved through him from the wrath of God. For if while we were enemies, we were reconciled to God through the death of his Son, much more surely, having been reconciled, will we be saved by his life. But more than that, we even boast in God through our Lord Jesus Christ, through whom we have now received reconciliation.

Colossians 1:15–23

[Jesus Christ] is the image of the invisible God, the firstborn of all creation; for in him all things in heaven and on earth were created, things visible and invisible, whether thrones or dominions or rulers or powers—all things have been created through him and for him. He himself is before all things, and in him all things hold together. He is the head of the body, the church; he is the beginning, the firstborn from the dead, so that he might come to have first place in everything. For in him all the fullness of God was pleased to dwell, and through him God was pleased to reconcile to himself all things, whether on earth or in heaven, by making peace through the blood of his cross.

And you who were once estranged and hostile in mind, doing evil deeds, he has now reconciled in his fleshly body through death, so as to present you holy and blameless and irreproachable before him— provided that you continue securely established and steadfast in the faith, without shifting from the hope promised by the gospel that you heard, which has been proclaimed to every creature under heaven. I, Paul, became a servant of this gospel.

2 Corinthians 5:14–21

For the love of Christ urges us on, because we are convinced that one has died for all; therefore all have died. And he died for all, so that those who live might live no longer for themselves, but for him who died and was raised for them.

From now on, therefore, we regard no one from a human point of view; even though we once knew Christ from a human point of view, we know him no longer in that way. So if anyone is in Christ, there is a new creation: everything old has passed away; see, everything has become new! All this is from God, who reconciled us to himself through Christ, and has given us the ministry of reconciliation; that is, in Christ God was reconciling the world to himself, not counting their trespasses against them, and entrusting the message of reconciliation to us. So we are ambassadors for Christ, since God is making his appeal through us; we entreat you on behalf of Christ, be reconciled to God. For our sake he made him to be sin who knew no sin, so that in him we might become the righteousness of God.

While these passages pose a number of interpretive challenges, three basic claims emerge clearly into view. First, reconciliation is a reality that establishes the possibility of subjective response. Second, reconciliation includes everyone. Third, one's subjective response to this objective reality is very important. The church has always emphasized the second two points. It knows that Christ was crucified and raised from the dead for everyone and that our response matters. But it has not consistently affirmed the first point—that reconciliation is a perfect reality—and its failure to do so has often led it to misconstrue the second two points.[6] Because unless you see that reconciliation is a fact that Jesus Christ accomplishes on his own, a truth that does not require a supplemental work from us to become

6. Reformed theologians who stress the reality of reconciliation but limit its scope are an obvious exception to this rule.

real, you will not adequately understand what it means to say that reconciliation includes everyone. And you will likely make the further mistake of thinking that our response, rather than Jesus Christ himself, is what ultimately reconciles us to God. But that is not how these passages work. God's reconciling love in Christ calls forth our response but is not contingent upon it. Our response does not create the relationship that sets us right with God. Jesus Christ does that. He alone reconciles the world to God. To be clear, I emphasize this crucial point not to deny the importance of our subjective response—which will become obvious in the next section and throughout the rest of the book—but because the church has often failed to perceive its truth and significance.

Becoming Who You Are

If what these passages declare is true, then the deepest question of human life has been answered. The most important thing that can be said about each and every one of us is that Jesus Christ has reconciled us to God. He "is the true life of humanity."[7] His grace, mercy, and compassion define us. In him God has established

7. CD 4.3.2:183, rev.

peace with us, and he continually calls us to live at peace with him, with our neighbors, and with ourselves. "The truth of our existence is simply this—that Jesus Christ has died and risen again for us. It is this and this alone which is to be proclaimed to us as our truth."[8] To his credit, Dietrich Bonhoeffer perceives the significance of this point for theological education: "Christian education begins where all other education ceases: What is essential *has already happened*."[9]

This way of thinking leads to a few obvious questions. If all of this is true, then why does our response matter? If reconciliation is already a reality, why was Paul willing to lose everything for the sake of this "ministry of reconciliation"? If we are already reconciled to God, why does Paul call us to "be reconciled to God"?

The first thing to say is that since reconciliation is restored relationship with God, and since faith and obedience are how we live in right relationship with God, the idea that reconciliation doesn't require our response is absurd. Of course it does; that's the whole

8. *CD* 2.1:167, rev.
9. *DBWE* 14:538. See also Bonhoeffer's comment, "The unique feature of Christian education, instruction, is that here persons *are* in essence already *that which they are to become*. . . . All Christian instruction must begin with this presupposition. All other education begins with the presupposition that the human being is to become what he is not yet" (*DBWE* 14:538).

point. Grace necessarily calls forth gratitude. God reconciles us *for* fellowship with him and one another. Rather than being an abstract fact that doesn't include us, or one that somehow makes our response irrelevant, objective reconciliation is a living reality whose goal is the transformation of human existence, indeed the transformation of "all things" (Col. 1:20). Our lives are "hidden with Christ in God" (Col. 3:3) *in order to be received and embraced.* That subjective response is how we become (in ourselves) who we already are (in Christ). When, in the power of the Spirit, we perceive this world-altering truth and respond to Jesus Christ in "simple obedience,"[10] our existence becomes analogous to his human existence, which is itself one extended act of faith and obedience. For all their dissimilarities, our lives become similar to his life. Thus the summons to discipleship is a summons to live with the grain of one's identity in Christ rather than against it. As this happens we become images of the image of God. Our existence, the shape of our individual lives, coheres with our essence in him.

It is important to notice that this is not a call to social conformity. Since Christ's command is personal

10. *DBWE* 4:77.

rather than generic, its shape and meaning differ from
person to person. His call for you to become who you
are is not identical to his call for me to become who
I am. We may assume they share a common unity—
since Jesus Christ is the one who calls both of us,
and he is the same yesterday, today, and forever—but
Christ's call is irreducibly personal. It comes "to each
individual in a highly particular way in one's own particular time and situation."[11] We discern and respond
to Christ's voice in community with others, but discipleship, the process whereby we become who we are,
is not something anyone else can do for us. "Jesus' call
to discipleship makes the disciple into a single individual. Whether disciples want to or not, they have to
make a decision; each has to decide alone."[12] And since
we receive ourselves as we respond to Christ in faith,
all of us have "the same essential task"[13]—namely, to
become who we are in him.

Conceiving of the human self as a process, as both a
gift and a task, implies that we are not simply ourselves

11. *CD* 4.2:547, rev.
12. *DBWE* 4:92. Bonhoeffer borrowed the term "single individual"
from Kierkegaard.
13. Søren Kierkegaard, *Three Discourses on Imagined Occasions*, ed.
and trans. Howard V. Hong and Edna H. Hong (Princeton: Princeton
University Press, 1993), 38.

in a straightforward way, nor do we become ourselves all at once. At best we are on the way toward becoming ourselves. At most our existence is in the process of becoming aligned with our essence. But this is a constant struggle. Discipleship never becomes automatic. If the Christian life were merely a matter of acquiring the right information, or a process of socialization into an established culture or set of behaviors, perhaps following Jesus could eventually become second nature. But Christ's call is unpredictable; it cannot be known before the fact. In the New Testament, more often than not, Christ's words and actions are met with surprise, even shock, and those who choose to follow him find themselves in continual "confrontation with the new and strange Jesus Christ."[14] Thus it seems reasonable to conclude that the lives of those who apprentice themselves to him will be characterized more by disruptive and surprising encounters than by stable and predictable configurations of life. To be clear, our identity in Christ is stable and unchanging, but the existential shape of life together with him is not.

Thus if our true humanity is hidden with Christ in God, and if we embrace that life in faith and obedience,

14. CD 4.3.1:183.

a fitting way to conceptualize Christian existence is to think of it as "eccentric existence."[15] Or as Bonhoeffer expresses this point, "For the Christian, 'being': 'be who you are,' comes from the outside."[16] To live in faith is to live outside oneself in union with Christ. Paul's great exclamation, "I have been crucified with Christ; and it is no longer I who live, but it is Christ who lives in me" (Gal. 2:19–20), implies that we are never more fully human, never more fully ourselves, never more free, than when our lives become transparent to the life of Christ. That is how the Spirit liberates us to become who we are—not by turning us into the kind of people who automatically know and do the good, but by granting us faith to entrust ourselves again and again to Christ, whose power is made perfect in our weakness. As Søren Kierkegaard expresses it in a formulation that cannot be improved upon: "The helper is the help."[17]

But Paul's language of co-crucifixion with Christ makes clear that the process whereby we gain our lives by losing them and receive our lives by giving them away often *feels* less like liberation than like being torn

15. *CD* 4.3.2:548.
16. *DBWE* 14:539.
17. Søren Kierkegaard, *Practice in Christianity*, ed. and trans. Howard V. Hong and Edna H. Hong (Princeton: Princeton University Press, 1991), 15.

apart. And in the midst of this struggle, we face the constant temptation to settle into comfortable patterns of life that insulate us from the threat of God's commanding grace. Resisting that temptation, living in faith, requires strenuous effort. That may sound paradoxical, especially to Protestants, but it shouldn't. God's grace is not opposed to working but to earning and to self-reliance. Kierkegaard expresses this point lucidly in an extraordinary journal entry, one that belies his caricature as a grim legalist: "If I were to define Christian perfection, I would not say that it is a perfection of striving, but that it is precisely the profound acknowledgment of the imperfection of one's striving, and therefore precisely a deeper and deeper consciousness of the need for grace, not in relation to one thing or another, but of the infinite need for infinite grace."[18]

Yet all too often we do not rely on grace. We refuse to receive our lives from Christ. We enter into conflict with him and thus into conflict with ourselves. When that happens, our existence contradicts our essence, and we somehow strangely become who we are not. Sin is entrance into a kind of nonbeing, into a form of life that has no future—one that has already been put

18. *KJN* 8:188.

to death with Christ. In other words, sin is absurd. It doesn't add up. It's like going to the track and betting your life's savings on a dead horse. It's God rescuing Israel from Egypt and Israel longing to return to slavery. It's receiving the gift of new life in Christ and preferring to labor under the impossible burden of trying to invent yourself. In a series of striking images, Barth and Kierkegaard describe sin as "falling out with oneself,"[19] being "at odds with oneself,"[20] becoming "a traitor to oneself,"[21] and "being untruth."[22] Thus sin is existence not only against God and neighbor but also against oneself. "Falling away from Christ," Bonhoeffer observes, "is at the same time falling away from one's own true nature."[23] Nevertheless, sin does not have the power to remake human nature. If God really has reconciled the world to himself in Christ, then nothing we do has the power to reverse that, and to understand our students, we have to recognize that every single one of

19. *CD* 4.2:570.

20. *CD* 4.2:570.

21. Søren Kierkegaard, *Eighteen Upbuilding Discourses*, ed. and trans. Howard V. Hong and Edna H. Hong (Princeton: Princeton University Press, 1990), 318.

22. Søren Kierkegaard, *Philosophical Fragments*, ed. and trans. Howard V. Hong and Edna H. Hong (Princeton: Princeton University Press, 1985), 15.

23. *DBWE* 6:134.

them is essentially defined by the love of God in Christ, not by their opposition to God's love.

The Holy Spirit: The Primary Teacher

As I suggested earlier, teachers are incapable of engineering faith in students. By the grace of God, our teaching sometimes participates in the movement of disturbance, awakening, and renewal through which students come to see and embrace who they are in Christ. But we are never in control of this process. If the truth is not something a teacher possesses, the truth is not something a teacher dispenses—no matter how gifted one happens to be. God alone reveals God. Thankfully God chooses to do so through human witnesses, but the effectiveness of our teaching depends ultimately on the presence and activity of the Holy Spirit. God is the primary teacher in our classrooms: "No one can say 'Jesus is Lord' except by the Holy Spirit" (1 Cor. 12:3). Thus our teaching will be successful, at least in the deepest sense of that word, only when the Spirit uses it to make God known to students.[24]

---

24. In *Philosophical Fragments*, Johannes Climacus raises the question, "Can the truth be learned?" He concludes that God must give both the truth and the condition for receiving the truth. I think he was right. See

Consider one among many pedagogical benefits implied in this claim. Many of us who teach Christian theology are keenly aware of the poverty of our language in comparison to the reality of God. We try our best to speak truthfully and faithfully, but our words often seem thin and unreal, they taste like ashes on our tongues, and we wonder if our teaching will add up to anything more than wasted time. In extreme cases, this trajectory of thought and feeling can lead to a deadening acedia that takes root within teachers and leaves us hopeless or in despair.[25] But an awareness of our dependence on the Spirit moves us in the opposite direction. It eases the pressure by displacing the teacher from the center of the educational process. It relativizes our weaknesses. It does not eliminate them, and it certainly does not excuse them, but it assures us that God rises above them. And this awareness becomes an essential source of freedom and joy for those who believe and depend on it, whereas for those who do not, teaching can become a burden too heavy to

---

Kierkegaard, *Philosophical Fragments*, 9–22. This passage is essential reading for anyone who teaches Christian theology.

25. Acedia, "the noonday demon," traditionally translated as "sloth," is a kind of spiritual boredom or apathy that leads to despair. For a penetrating discussion, see Evagrius Ponticus, *The Praktikos and Chapters on Prayer*, trans. John Eudes Bamberger (Kalamazoo, MI: Cistercian Publications, 1972), 18–26.

bear—at least for teachers who want their students to know God personally. Our confidence that God will reveal himself to students is grounded not in our own competence, character, or powers of persuasion, but in God's desire to be known and in the "eloquent and radiant" presence of the risen Christ, who makes himself known in the power of the Spirit.[26]

Prayer

If this is true, if knowledge of God and the obedience of faith are gifts of divine grace, then prayer is the sine qua non of teaching Christian theology—the essential pedagogical practice. Teaching in a context that does not permit public prayer is certainly not an exception to this rule, since in that case one would simply pray in silence and outside of class. No matter the context, the effectiveness of our teaching depends ultimately on a movement of the Spirit of God. Kierkegaard's observation about the Christian life in general certainly applies to teaching Christian theology: "to need God is our highest perfection."[27]

26. *CD* 4.3.1:79. See also Barth's comment, "What can all our Christian statements be but a serious pointing away to the One who will himself tell those who have ears to hear who he is?" (*CD* 4.1:210).

27. Kierkegaard, *Eighteen Upbuilding Discourses*, 312, rev.

But we must also reckon with the fact that the Spirit does not have to move in our classes. While our need is absolute, God is under no obligation to make use of our teaching. To assume otherwise is to presume upon his grace.[28] Which means that there is nothing more urgent for teachers to do than to pray for the coming of the Holy Spirit—especially when what we are asking for is "the wondrous thing, that people's blind eyes and deaf ears may be opened."[29] And notice—not merely to *think* about praying, or to agree that praying would be a good idea, but actually to spend time asking the Spirit to act in our classes.[30]

Consider the pedagogical implications of this insight. The freedom of the Spirit of God implies that there are no fail-safe strategies capable of guaranteeing success in the classroom, no foolproof rhetorical methods for us to learn, and certainly no "instruments" for quantitatively assessing the effectiveness of our teaching that would appease the accreditors. No matter how

28. According to Barth, "A presupposed spirit is certainly not the Holy Spirit, and a theology that assumes to have it under control could only be unspiritual theology" (*ET*, 58).

29. *ET*, 169.

30. See Augustine's perfect formulation: "Let one be a pray-er before being a speaker" (*The Works of Saint Augustine: A Translation for the 21st Century*, ed. John E. Rotelle, vol. 11, *Teaching Christianity*, trans. Edmund Hill [Hyde Park, NY: New City Press, 1996], 226, rev.).

skilled or industrious we are, there is no guarantee that our teaching will amount to anything more than wasted time. What worked yesterday might not work today, and what works tomorrow might never work again.[31] A theologian "cannot continue to build today in any way on foundations that were laid yesterday by himself, and he cannot live today in any way on the interest from a capital amassed yesterday. His only possible procedure every day, in fact, every hour, is to begin again at the beginning."[32] To use this as a pretext for excusing pedagogical incompetence would be to miss the point entirely. Of course pedagogy matters; everyone knows that. But competence alone is not enough, since "unless the LORD builds the house, those who build it labor in vain" (Ps. 127:1). Thus progress in the art of teaching Christianity necessarily includes progress in the art of prayer.

---

31. See Bonhoeffer's comment, "There are no Christian educational ideals, educational models, but only the call to discipleship at a certain point. It is left to *God* to shape the person according to *God's likeness*. Any restriction of Christian education to an ideal truncates its task. God alone is given the freedom to create God's image within the person" (*DBWE* 14:540).

32. *ET*, 165.

2

KNOWLEDGE

Some of the best theology students I know do not believe in God. This should not be surprising, since one obviously does not need to believe in God to perform well in an academic course. Compared to Christian students who hold badly informed or deeply misguided views about God, students who do not believe in God often have less to unlearn. When they encounter new theological ideas, many respond with penetrating questions and fresh insights that don't occur to most students long familiar with the same ideas. The point is not to romanticize such people. I have taught plenty of terrible students who do not believe in God. The point is that they performed terribly not because they do not believe in God but because they either could not or would not do the necessary academic work. To avoid misunderstanding what follows, I ask readers to please keep all of this clearly in mind. In an academic context, teachers evaluate only academic work. It is not our responsibility to assess the existential transformation that occurs (or does not occur) in students as they study Christian theology. Indeed, we could not reliably do so even if we wanted to.

Understanding and Existence

Reflecting back on his prolific career as a writer, Søren Kierkegaard claims that the "fundamental idea" of his authorship as a whole was the question of "what it means to become a Christian."[1] Describing his decision to dedicate his life to this question, Kierkegaard writes, "Even if I never managed to become a Christian, I would before God employ all my time and all my diligence at least to get it made clear what Christianity is."[2] Everyone who teaches Christian theology shares this same basic task. It is not possible to teach the Christian faith seriously, responsibly, or professionally without attempting to clarify what Christianity is.

1. Søren Kierkegaard, *The Point of View*, ed. and trans. Howard V. Hong and Edna H. Hong (Princeton: Princeton University Press, 1998), 92.

2. Kierkegaard, *Point of View*, 93.

Whatever one's theological sensibilities, and however one approaches the work, this requirement is inescapable. It is also extremely difficult. And one of the most subtle and tenacious obstacles to clarifying the meaning of the Christian faith is the tendency—in teachers and students alike—to lose sight of the difference between knowing theology and knowing God. As students encounter the capacious world of Christian theology, as they become familiar with its shape and contours, as they perceive its order, beauty, and depth (along with its disorder, pettiness, and confusion), as they encounter its greatest minds and struggle to understand and assess its central affirmations, they easily conflate cognitive agreement with Christian faith. They confuse believing in God with believing ideas about God. Furthermore, many do not realize this is happening, which makes the problem even worse. Sometimes this pathology mirrors one that exists in their teachers, and even when that is not the case, our instruction contributes to the problem whenever we teach without an abiding awareness of the difference between knowing God and knowing about God. Failing to communicate this to students, or placing the accent so strongly on intellectual comprehension that students unwittingly confuse thinking with existing, are two of the easiest mistakes teachers make, and two of the most subtle ways we misrepresent Christianity.

To be clear, knowing God includes knowing about God: "*Pistis* [faith] says more than *gnosis* [knowledge] but in all circumstances it says *gnosis* too."[3] But knowing God cannot be reduced to knowing about God, since "knowledge in the biblical sense directly includes, indeed it is itself at root, *metanoia*, conversion, the transformation of the *nous* [mind], and therefore of the whole person."[4] A detached and purely objective knowledge of God, even if it were possible, would be incomplete. The truth is known only when it takes up residence in a person's life, when it begins to express itself in and through that person. As Karl Barth writes, "We cannot impress upon ourselves too strongly that in the language of the Bible knowledge (*yada*, γιγνώσκειν) does not mean the acquisition of neutral information, which can be expressed in statements, principles and systems. . . . We can and should say even more emphatically that knowledge in the biblical sense is the process in which the distant 'object' dissolves as it were, overcoming both its distance and its objectivity and coming to a person as acting Subject, entering into

3. *CD* 1.1:229.
4. *CD* 4.3.1:185, rev.

the person who knows and subjecting that person to this transformation."[5]

Kierkegaard famously launched a blistering attack against teachers who give the false impression that living as a Christian can be reduced to thinking the right thoughts about God. According to the New Testament, Jesus Christ wants followers, not admirers, and while following him involves thinking about him, thinking about him is not yet following him. The truth offers us a new vantage point on our lives; it discloses new ways of existing. But envisioning new patterns of life is not the same as living them. Jesus Christ seeks disciples, not dilettantes. Since he is both the truth and the way, to know him you have to commit yourself to him. Given the destructive consequences that result from inattention to the difference between knowing theology and knowing God, Kierkegaard mercilessly derides teachers who lose sight of this. He writes that "doctrine is what people want. Because doctrine is easy imitation for the student, and doctrine is palpable

---

5. CD 4.3.1:183–84, rev. See also Bonhoeffer's comment that "knowledge cannot be separated from the existence in which it was acquired" (*DBWE* 4:51). To mention one among many examples from Scripture, notice the relationship between obedience and knowledge in Jesus's statement, "If you continue in my word, you are truly my disciples; and you will know the truth, and the truth will make you free" (John 8:31–32).

power for the teacher."[6] He sketches a "preposterous comedy" in which "the apostle Paul is tested in theology by a theology professor," only to fail because "an apostle wouldn't know how to answer many of the questions from the catechism."[7] He compares the scholarly world of theology to a horse race in which riders "rush past one another, yell and shout, laugh and make fools of one another, drive their horses to death, tip over and are run over, and when they finally reach [the finish line] covered in dust and out of breath—yes, then they look at one another—and go home."[8] And he unforgettably observes that "if a lark wants to fart like an elephant, it will end up bursting. And in the same way, scholarly theology will also burst because instead of being what it is—a modest triviality—it wants to be the supreme form of wisdom."[9]

Anyone who has ever been to an academic theology conference knows what Kierkegaard is talking about. Personally, I cannot get passages like these out of my head. Once you internalize them, they begin to influence everything you say in the classroom. It would be a mistake to draw the conclusion that Kierkegaard rejected

6. *KJN* 10:189.
7. *KJN* 6:54.
8. *KJN* 1:18.
9. *KJN* 6:52.

the basic doctrinal affirmations of the Christian faith. He ridiculed the abuse of Christian doctrine, indeed Christian doctrine itself to the extent that it becomes an impediment to offering oneself completely to God, but his authorship would be unintelligible apart from the confession that Jesus Christ is both divine and human. Kierkegaard's fight was not with Christian doctrine per se but with the misuse of doctrine to support an intellectualized Christianity that evades the demands of discipleship.[10] To know God, one must commit oneself to God in such a way that one's life "reduplicates" the truth.[11] If God were an object in the world, or an idea, or a principle of logic, that would not be the case. There is nothing inherently contradictory about a biologist making a breakthrough discovery while pulling the wings off a butterfly. But one cannot simultaneously know God while refusing to offer oneself to God. To suggest otherwise is to misunderstand who God is, or what it means

10. See Kierkegaard's comment, "In general, the doctrine, as it is presented, is entirely sound. Thus I am not fighting against that. My contention is that something should follow from this" (*KJN* 8:113). See also his claim, "The doctrines of the established order, its organization, are very good. Ah, but the lives, our lives—believe me, they are mediocre. . . . Our lives are only slightly touched by the doctrine" (*KJN* 8:219).

11. Søren Kierkegaard, *Practice in Christianity*, ed. and trans. Howard V. Hong and Edna H. Hong (Princeton: Princeton University Press, 1991), 134.

to know God, or both. The goal of theological study is not merely to understand but to "exist in what one understands."[12] It is not a mark of academic seriousness to sever contemplation from action, intellect from existence, reason from affections, or thinking from living. These terms become disconnected from one another only when one forgets what Christianity is.

And yet it seems to me that many of us who teach Christian theology are better and more comfortable helping students "look at" Christian doctrines than helping them "look along" them—better at helping students understand theological ideas and arguments than helping them reflect on the difference theology makes for life.[13] In many university and seminary classes, we fix our attention so strongly on the descriptive task of

12. Kierkegaard, *Practice in Christianity*, 134. An important distinction needs to be made here. To say that God is known subjectively in faith is not to fall into subjectivism. Faith does not make God real. Whereas we depend on God to be who we are, God does not depend on us to be who he is. Kierkegaard's well-known claim that "truth is subjectivity" is an observation about how truth is received, known, and lived, not an endorsement of epistemological subjectivism. Kierkegaard would have agreed with Barth's claim that the truth "would be the truth even if it had no witnesses. It is the truth even though all its human witnesses fail. It does not live by Christians, Christians live by it" (*CD* 4.3.2:656).

13. The distinction between "looking at" and "looking along" comes from C. S. Lewis's essay "Meditation in a Toolshed," in *God in the Dock: Essays on Theology and Ethics*, ed. Walter Hooper (Grand Rapids: Eerdmans, 1970), 230–34.

clarifying theological content that we neglect to help students explore theology's existential implications. Rather than envisioning these tasks as inseparably related to each another, the latter becomes an after-thought, if not a practice altogether out of place in an academic context. To understand how this problem arose, we need to take a brief glance at the development of academic theology.

Excursus: The Development of Academic Theology

Prior to the Middle Ages, Christian theology was written and taught primarily by church leaders and monks whose basic task was to reflect on Scripture and the mysteries of the faith in order to serve the church and its ministry. Even those theologians who operated at the most technical and sophisticated levels shared an essentially pastoral aim: to guide the church into the truth of the gospel and to equip Christians to live more faithfully and intelligently as disciples of Jesus Christ. Whether responding to critics, instructing new converts, clarifying difficult questions, or seeking deeper insight into the meaning and implications of the Christian message, theological work intended to instruct and illuminate the church, offering Christians intellectual and spiritual guidance in their attempts to know and follow Jesus Christ. This instruction occurred in a wide array of forms and contexts, but it was inseparably related to Christian existence in the world.

As theologians moved into the newly formed universities of the Middle Ages, their reflection, writing, and teaching were affected by this transition. Professors were clergy who remained under the authority of Scripture and the church, but the university offered them an expanding range of sources upon which to draw and a broader set of conversations in which to engage. The result was "a great surge in theological studies that has no parallel in the entire history of Christianity."[14] An important feature of this transition is that "university studies became increasingly specialized but at the same time increasingly distant from parochial life as well as from the interests of those who practiced pastoral ministry."[15] To be sure, university students and professors "devoted themselves to theological studies on the basis of a firm commitment to the Christian faith and a profound conviction that their studies would help them grow in faith."[16] Nevertheless, "it is clear that

14. Justo González, *The History of Theological Education* (Nashville: Abingdon, 2015), 52.
15. González, *History of Theological Education*, 47.
16. González, *History of Theological Education*, 47.

much of the theology that was studied, discussed, and produced in the universities had no great relevance to ministerial practice" or the life of ordinary believers.[17] This is not a criticism. Some of the most intellectually exciting and spiritually rich theological writings ever produced by the church emerged from the pens of these scholars, and their enduring value, as well as their influence on the development of Western intellectual history, is incalculable. But the movement into the context of the medieval university does mark an important phase in a gradual parting of the ways between academic theological scholarship and the life of the church—a division that would in the modern period harden into estrangement.

Like so many developments in modern theology, this estrangement is inseparably related to the history of theology in Germany.[18] Theology in the modern German university was to be a form of science (*Wissenschaft*), which, like other sciences, needed to justify its place within the university curriculum, and thus

17. González, *History of Theological Education*, 51.
18. For this history, see Thomas Albert Howard, *Protestant Theology and the Making of the Modern German University* (Oxford: Oxford University Press, 2006); and Zachary Purvis, *Theology and the University in Nineteenth-Century Germany*, Oxford Theology and Religion Monographs (Oxford: Oxford University Press, 2016).

found itself accountable to the reigning norms of secular reason. In this situation, theological scholarship could no longer appeal to authorities such as Scripture and tradition, and instead had to subject them (along with every other supposed authority) to the bar of critical reason. Whether a particular scholar intended his or her work to strengthen the life of the church, in order to count as legitimate scholarship, indeed to count as knowledge, one's work had to answer to the same rational standards as every other academic discipline. Under these conditions, theologians could no longer presuppose the truth of the gospel. If Christian theology wanted to be accepted as a responsible form of intellectual inquiry, it would have to submit itself to a supposedly universal and objective standard of rationality, one that floats above any specific context or tradition, even when doing so precludes primary Christian affirmations. In such circumstances, modern theology inevitably struggled to remain connected to its subject matter. Moreover—and for our purposes this is the most important point—its primary audience had shifted from the church to the academy. A scholar may happen to be personally concerned with the Christian faith, even offer one's critical scholarship in service of the church, but such commitments had become optional. It was now perfectly acceptable to go about one's academic writing and teaching unconcerned with its influence on the life of the church or its value for Christian existence.[19]

Envisioning Existence

Returning now to our previous discussion, if Barth and Kierkegaard are correct that knowing God is a way of life, then our task cannot be merely descriptive. We have the additional responsibility to help students envision the existential implications of the doctrines we present—to help them discover what it might mean for their lives to express and bear witness to the truth. Yet few things are easier than ignoring or neglecting this work. For years I taught without even attempting to do this. I convinced myself that wasting precious class time exploring the personal implications of Christian theology was too homiletical, too academically unserious. Now I see things differently. Now I understand

19. For the record, this excursus is descriptive rather than evaluative. Like the inheritance of medieval theology, modern theology offers an ocean of invaluable, even essential, resources, many of which I draw upon in this book and for which every Christian theologian ought to be grateful. I sketch this history not to disparage modern theology but to contextualize the division between intellect and existence that pervades contemporary theological education.

that those were pretexts designed to disguise moral and intellectual cowardice—flimsy excuses to let myself off the hook, to protect myself against criticism, and to compensate for incompetence. I assumed that if I could present Christian doctrines clearly and compellingly, students would somehow, without any guidance from me, grasp their existential significance. And while I'm sure some of them did, I conveniently convinced myself that academic rigor and professionalism precluded me from helping them with this creative work. I decided it was off-limits to explore topics like the incoherence between our explicit beliefs and our default patterns of life, the countless ways Western culture applies pressure on us to become protean personalities, how our families form and deform us, the incompatibility between the broad narrative of Scripture and the background narratives that guide our lives, and so on. But the real reason I didn't discuss such subjects is now clear to me: I simply had no clue how to help students think along these lines—no idea how to help them engage in the art of theological imagination. And so I didn't.

But this is precisely the kind of guidance most of our students are seeking, at least until academia conditions them to forget why they became interested in God in the first place. Most students want to know what it means

to live well and to help others live well, and they expect
our courses to help them clarify their allegiances. "The
human condition is such that you have to choose how
to live from among options that rule one another out."[20]
That has always been the case, but during times of rapid
cultural change, the range of competing visions of the
good broadens, and contradictory ways of thinking and
living multiply and exist alongside one another. During
such periods, the need to consciously decide what to
believe and how to live becomes more pressing and more
difficult. In a pluralistic context, committing oneself passionately to one option among many may seem arbitrary,
irrational, and absurd, but the inevitable alternative is to
drift along in the current of contemporary society and
thus away from a life of integrity and coherence. While
many of our students would struggle to diagnose and articulate this dilemma, they experience it intensely. They
report feeling fragmented, scattered, divided against
themselves, and strangely paralyzed by our chaotic and
confusing culture. They want to live meaningful lives,
and they abhor the idea of "settling," but they struggle to
know what it means to live well as they navigate a sea of
incompatible possibilities, and they expect us to help.

20. C. Kavin Rowe, *One True Life: The Stoics and Early Christians as
Rival Traditions* (New Haven: Yale University Press, 2016), 1.

Yet it is precisely here that teachers are tempted to commit an error as harmful as the one I've been describing. As students seek clarity and insight, teachers easily fall into the trap of posing as all-knowing oracles, experts with all the answers. Not only is projecting this image ridiculous; it also betrays a basic misunderstanding of our relationship to students. The moment we begin to operate as quasi-omniscient gurus, experts with the solution to every problem, we exchange teaching for propaganda, instruction for demagoguery, the Word of God for our words about God. God does not call us to offer definitive counsel to our students, as if we could somehow anticipate what God is saying to each one of them personally, as if we know what shape the truth will take in their lives. Nor does God instruct us to deposit definitive theological formulations into their minds. (Are we really so benighted as to think we could do either of these things anyway?) We are responsible for thinking with students, not for them. To do otherwise is to confuse education with indoctrination. And while some students will want to hand their freedom over to us—after all, it is far easier when someone else thinks for you—allowing them to do so is lethal to theological education.

To be sure, this approach is risky. Once students start thinking for themselves—under the lordship of Christ, and within the communion of saints, but on their own two feet—teachers have less control over where students will end up.[21] But control is an illusion anyway. And besides, are we really so convinced that our perceptions of the truth are superior to those God will lead our students to discover? Would we really want to fix our ideas in their minds even if we could? As Barth once observed, "There is no theology without risk."[22] Indeed, how could there be, when theological reflection is an aspect of Christian discipleship? We cannot think about Jesus from a safe distance any more than we can follow him from a safe distance. And while attaching ourselves to him is dangerous, so too is seeking safety in the crowd, or in timeless formulas, or in a teacher who does our thinking for us.

Two Objections and Two Replies

Before moving to the next chapter, I would like to briefly address two objections that, if present in the minds of readers, will likely call this entire discussion

21. Thus to think for oneself is obviously not to think by oneself.
22. *CD* 4.2:10.

into question. Many of the Christian students who take my classes arrive with the assumption that God is unknowable. They assume that because God is mysterious, God cannot be known, and they express this conviction in a standard formula: "You cannot put God in a box." It seems to me that this way of thinking usually proceeds from a sincere desire to honor God and to be appropriately humble. Students assume that God is greater if God cannot be known and thus to claim otherwise would be arrogant and misguided. Thankfully, many of them hold this belief alongside another belief that moves in the opposite direction—namely, that Jesus Christ is God's definitive self-disclosure. But if it is true that anyone who has seen Jesus has seen the Father (John 14:9), if he is the image of the invisible God (Col. 1:15), if the fullness of deity dwells bodily in him (Col. 2:9), if he is the Lord (Phil. 2:9–11) and makes God known (John 1:18), then God can be known. If God makes himself known, then God can be known.[23] The reality of knowledge of God establishes the possibility of knowledge of God. Thus the assumption that God is unknowable, while

---

23. Moreover, God is knowable because the Father and Son know each other in the unity of the Spirit. Our knowledge of God occurs as God graciously allows us to participate in his triune self-knowledge in a form that is appropriate to us as creatures.

sincere, is not an expression of genuine humility. After all, if Jesus reveals God, who are we to say God cannot be known? How would such a belief square with the trustworthiness of God's self-revelation in Christ? Besides, if God were unknowable, he would not be able to reveal himself even if he wanted to do so, which would detract from his greatness rather than increase it.

Of course God is mysterious. The students are right about that. But the key to thinking about divine mystery in a specifically Christian way—in a way that doesn't result in agnosticism about God and isn't merely an affirmation of the limits of our natural understanding—is to notice that divine mystery is *revealed* in Jesus Christ. The mystery of the triune God is not a general and abstract concept, but a reality we learn from Jesus Christ, who is himself "God's mystery . . . in whom are hidden all the treasures of wisdom and knowledge" (Col. 2:2–3). Of course, there is more than a grain of truth in the idea that God cannot be known. We know God only because God wants us to know him; had God chosen not to reveal himself to us, we would not know him. It is also true that we do not fully comprehend God; we do not know God as God knows himself. Our knowledge is limited and fallible. But those are descriptions of our knowledge of God, not denials of our knowledge of God. They are affirmations that our knowledge of God is a gift of divine grace and that it occurs within limits, not that it doesn't occur at all.

But this leads to another objection. Even if we grant that knowledge of God is possible, how do we distinguish between the real God and the many false gods generated by our own thoughts and desires? Everyone is susceptible to error, no matter how earnest, virtuous, or intelligent that person happens to be. The distortions of our character and the limitations of our finitude cloud and confuse our perception. We become convinced that truth is falsehood and falsehood is truth. We see what we want to see, or what we think we see, even when it does not really exist. As Thom Yorke put it: "Just 'cause you feel it, doesn't mean it's there."[24] But then how do we know God is not a figment of our imagination? How do we know we're not just dreaming him up?

The first point to acknowledge is that our ideas about God might be wrong. It is always possible to fall into theological error. Barth's most important contribution to the history of Christian theology—his

24. From "There, There," track 9 on Radiohead, *Hail to the Thief*, Capitol Records, 2003, compact disc.

breathtaking attempt to allow Jesus Christ to be the center and norm of all Christian reflection—emerged out of a keen awareness of how sentimental, misguided, self-indulgent, harmful, and evil our conceptions of God often are. Consider, for example, his response to Ludwig Feuerbach. Feuerbach launched a penetrating argument against religion, accusing it of being a disguised form of anthropology. You may think you're talking about God, Feuerbach argued, but you're really only talking about yourselves. God does not exist. Theology is nothing more than the projection of human desires, fears, powers, and so on. To his enduring credit, Barth recognized that Feuerbach had given the church a profound gift.[25] In Barth's estimation, Feuerbach was right; much of our thinking does fall prey to his critique, which means the only way beyond Feuerbach is through him. For the church to avoid the mistake of confusing theology with anthropology, confusing talk about God with talk about ourselves, its

---

25. Kierkegaard was similarly appreciative. In his opinion, Feuerbach was "defending Christianity against the present generation of Christians. . . . It is indeed a falsehood when established Christendom says that Feuerbach attacks Christianity—that is not true, he is attacking the Christians by showing that their lives do not correspond to the teaching of Christianity. This is infinitely different" (*KJN* 6:339). In a marvelous turn of phrase, Kierkegaard described Feuerbach as a "godly traitor," someone who, despite his atheism, was "absolutely loyal" to God (*KJN* 6:340).

thinking must be governed at every point by God's own self-revelation in Christ. "Jesus Christ, as he is attested to us in Holy Scripture, is the one Word of God whom we have to hear, and whom we have to trust and obey in life and in death."[26] To the extent that Christian theology loses sight of him, or submits itself to some other criterion, it wanders into the dark.

If Barth is correct about this, then learning Christian theology is a process of learning to read reality in the light of Christ—learning to "take every thought captive to obey Christ" (2 Cor. 10:5).[27] As the Word of God becomes the living criterion of our speech about God—a criterion we neither possess nor control— familiar ideas become untenable, startling new ones emerge, and theological reflection proceeds along surprising trajectories. As the cross and resurrection become for us "the axiom of all axioms," as our default patterns of thought are transformed in light of the fact that God became a man who died in the first century and is currently alive today, we learn to be suspicious

26. *CD* 2.1:172—quoting the Barmen Declaration. See also *CD* 4.1:346.

27. "Within theological thinking generally, unconditional priority must be given to thinking which is attentive to the existence of the living person of Jesus Christ" (*CD* 4.3.1:175). To be clear, while Jesus Christ is the unifying center of Christian theology, Christian theology is obviously not exclusively about him.

of our common-sense theological assumptions and expectations, and we come to recognize that God is far stranger than we ever would have imagined.[28]

It is important to notice that accepting Jesus Christ as the criterion of our knowledge of God does not require us to reject extra-biblical or extra-Christian sources of wisdom. Why would it? It means, rather, that the church seeks to test all of its thinking against him. Christian faith is not opposed to reason or experience or any other source of wisdom. Knowledge of God is not esoteric or irrational. The God who fully and definitively reveals himself in Christ is free to reveal himself to whomever he pleases, and to do so through whatever means he pleases. Only hubris, ignorance, or ingratitude would lead anyone to think otherwise. Indeed, because God is alive, and because God loves the whole world, and because God desires to be known, we should expect him to reveal himself widely—and we should be happy when he does.

28. CD 4.1:346.

3

ETHOS

I f you teach Christianity, you need to read Karl Barth's
Evangelical Theology. Less explosive than his epoch-
making Romans commentaries, less daring and comprehensive than his magnum opus *Church Dogmatics*,
Evangelical Theology nevertheless exhibits, in its own
small way, the same level of quality as those more famous works. When the book was published in 1963,
Barth had been at the center of the academic theological
world for decades,[1] and *Evangelical Theology* turned
out to be his last great discussion of what it means
to be a Christian theologian. Fascinatingly, the book
is as concerned with what Barth called "theological
existence," the lives of theologians themselves, as it is
with questions of doctrine or theological method. In

---

1. During this period, Pope Pius XII called Barth the greatest theologian since Thomas Aquinas.

this chapter, I discuss our ethos as teachers, our credibility in the classroom, and I know no better way to approach this topic than by drawing attention to a few lines of thought in Barth's remarkable little book.

Diagnosis

Earlier, when I mentioned the important role *Evangelical Theology* played in my education as a teacher, I didn't explain what the book taught me. It was not Barth's theology; I had already written a book about the *Church Dogmatics*. What seized my attention was Barth's penetrating diagnosis of a spiritual disease that threatens everyone who teaches Christian theology. Alongside the bright and joyful major chord of Barth's reflections on the "happy science" of Christian theology, a darker and more ominous minor chord emerges.[2] If the good news is that God sometimes mercifully allows our theological work to become useful, the bad news is that theologians can become sick unto death, and all our exertions can add up to nothing. Instead of bearing witness to the light of life, instead of mirroring the truth in our own imperfect ways, our very existence can become darkness, and all our theological

2. *ET*, 16.

huffing and puffing can turn to poison. If you've ever read the book, you know I'm not exaggerating Barth's point. *Evangelical Theology* contains something like an MRI of a sick theologian and a warning that the disease is both contagious and terminal.

Theological existence animated by the fresh air of God's Spirit is a life of freedom, and Barth gives us a connoisseur's appreciation of the distinctive pleasures of the vocation. But alongside that, and just as clearly, he repeatedly warns us that our work can go horribly wrong. "Good" theology, he writes, is theology that is "pleasing to God and helpful to people,"[3] whereas bad theology, theology unanimated by the Spirit of God, is pestilential.

> It is clear that evangelical theology itself can only be pneumatic, spiritual theology. Only in the realm of the power of the Spirit can theology be realized as a humble, free, critical, and happy science of the God of the gospel. . . . Unspiritual theology, whether it works its woe in the pulpit or from the rostrum, on the printed page or in "discussions" among old or young theologians, would be one of the most terrible of all terrible occurrences on this earthly vale. It would be so bad as to be without comparison with the works of even the

3. *ET*, 196.

worst political journalist or the most wretched novels or films. Theology becomes unspiritual when it lets itself be enticed or evicted from the freshly flowing air of the Spirit of the Lord in which it can prosper.[4]

As you make your way through Barth's book, it begins to dawn on you that he is worried about us. Like a father fretting over his children, Barth knows how easy it is for theologians to veer off track, to waste our lives, and to do profound harm. And in *Evangelical Theology* he is trying as hard as he can to help us avoid that fate.

The love of God in Christ is the model of all good theological work. That is Barth's basic thesis: "If the object of theological knowledge is Jesus Christ and, in him, perfect love, then Agape alone can be the dominant and formative prototype and principle of theology."[5] Yet who among us would claim to consistently meet this standard? It is one thing to agree that teaching ought to be an act of self-emptying love on behalf of students, but quite another to teach that way. And while each of us falls short of this ideal in our own ways, Barth draws our attention to an especially corrosive vice that commonly infects us. The illness presents

4. *ET*, 55–56.
5. *ET*, 203.

as, among other things, an excessive concern for our reputations; a morbid craving for praise; a narcissistic pretentiousness combined with insecurity; a relentless desire to outdo our colleagues and to broadcast our accomplishments; a loveless envy when others succeed; and a gloomy anxiety about our legacies, about how people will remember and evaluate us when we're dead. The vice, of course, is vanity, and Barth considers it a menacing threat to theologians.

To put it simply, Barth thinks a vain theologian is an embodied contradiction of the gospel and the very antithesis of Jesus Christ himself. And he doesn't care how obvious this is. Barth doesn't care that making fun of self-important theologians is by now a tired cliché. He knows that vanity disables us, and because of that he is willing to sound the alarm. And we would do well not to evade his critique by dismissing it as moralistic or judgmental or whatever. He writes,

> What exegesis, sermon, or theological treatise is worthy of being called "good"? And is it not obviously sheer nonsense to speak of "famous" theologians or even theological "geniuses," not to mention considering oneself as such?[6]

6. *ET*, 150.

The genesis and existence of some great theologian? Nonsense—because what can "great" mean? There may be great lawyers, doctors, natural scientists, historians, and philosophers. But there are none other than little theologians, a fact that, incidentally, is fundamental to the "existentials" of theology.[7]

It might be thought that the statement, "Look how they love one another!" . . . might apply pre-eminently to theologians. But, in fact, theologians are nearly proverbial for their zealousness about all that they continually have in their hearts and on their lips to say against one another, and for what they put in black and white against one another with deep mistrust and a massive air of superiority.[8]

Ambition makes you look pretty ugly.[9]

Actually the last one is a line from Radiohead's album *OK Computer*, but it succinctly expresses Barth's point, and he certainly would have approved the formulation.

7. *ET*, 77.
8. *ET*, 139.
9. "Paranoid Android," track 2 on Radiohead, *OK Computer*, Capitol Records, 1997, compact disc.

It is tempting to interpret passages like these as nothing more than Barth's way of deflecting the ocean of praise that was being directed at him toward the end of his life. He was, after all, the most famous theologian in the world. When he traveled to America to give the first five lectures in *Evangelical Theology*, *Time* magazine put him on its cover. Or perhaps one sees in these statements a tacit admission that Barth did not always manage to live up to his own standards, and that is certainly true.[10] But Barth is aiming these passages at us too, and only an instinct for self-protection would lead us to think otherwise. Because if he wasn't troubled by our desire for greatness, he wouldn't aggressively remind us that we are nothing more than "little theologians." He wouldn't criticize us for being more interested in the question "Who is the greatest among us?" than we are in the "plain and modest question about the matter at hand."[11] If he wasn't worried about the way we inflate ourselves by demeaning our rivals, he wouldn't

10. At this point, readers familiar with Barth's relationship with Charlotte von Kirschbaum will likely have in mind additional failures in Barth's personal life. For a judicious discussion of these matters, see Christiane Tietz, "Karl Barth and Charlotte von Kirschbaum," *Theology Today* 74, no. 2 (July 2017): 86–111.

11. *ET*, 139.

ask why there are "so many really woeful theologians who go around with faces that are eternally troubled or even embittered, always in a rush to bring forward their critical reservations and negations?"[12] And he wouldn't keep reminding us that evangelical theology is modest theology if he wasn't distressed by our immodesty—by the serenely confident way we make definitive pronouncements, even as we theoretically agree that all theological speech is limited and subject to revision. You don't write passages like the ones in this book unless you are concerned by how easily theologians confuse zealous pursuit of the truth with zealous pursuit of their own glory. It would not be far off to say that Barth's examination of this theme is something like a gloss on Jesus's claim that you cannot simultaneously work for praise from God and praise from people. You can seek one or the other, but not both.

It is important to see that Barth is not taking cheap shots at theologians here. Yes, he is giving us strong medicine, but he is giving it to us because he thinks vanity turns us into the kind of people whose lives obscure the truth—people who make the gospel less

12. *ET*, 94.

rather than more plausible.[13] We cannot, of course, make the gospel less true. God is God, and the truth is the truth, and nothing we do can change that. But Barth understands the role that the existence of the community plays in both the perception and concealment of truth. "The community does not speak with words alone," he writes. "It speaks by the very fact of its existence in the world."[14] There's what we say, and then there's who we are, and who we are says something.

And the connection with teaching is obvious. We believe that God sometimes uses flawed and sinful people like ourselves to make himself known. Since those are the only kind of people there are, those are the kind God uses. But how compelling could it possibly be for our students to hear us say, for example, that the Christian life is a life of self-giving that conforms to Jesus Christ's own life, or that the church lives to point away from itself to its Lord, when at the same time they see us carefully managing our CVs, ambitiously seeking acclaim and advancement, and morbidly competing with one another in exactly the same cutthroat ways

13. Søren Kierkegaard, of course, agreed: "Those who address the crowd, desiring its approval, those who most deferentially bow and scrape before it," he writes, are "instruments of untruth" (*KJN* 4:127, rev.).

14. *ET*, 38.

that people in every academic discipline compete with
one another? It doesn't add up. Arcade Fire is right:
it's absurd to trust a millionaire quoting the Sermon
on the Mount.[15] And it's no less absurd for students
to trust vain theologians when they talk about a crucified God.

I know this is not everyone's problem. Some readers
don't need to hear this. They struggle with other vices.
But anyone who has read the Gospels knows that Jesus
goes out of his way to address this problem. Speaking
specifically about teachers, he says, "They do all their
deeds to be seen by others. . . . They love to have the
place of honor at banquets and the best seats . . . and
to be greeted with respect . . . and to have people call
them [teacher]. . . . [But] the greatest among you will be
your servant. All who exalt themselves will be humbled,
and all who humble themselves will be exalted" (Matt.
23:1–12). In Luke 14 Jesus tells his disciples that following him requires giving up their possessions, and for
many of us, the possession we covet most, the thing we
cling to like greedy misers, is our reputation.

At this point a number of obvious questions arise.
Don't other people's opinions of us matter? Shouldn't

---

15. "City with No Children," track 6 on Arcade Fire, *Suburbs*, Merge
Records, 2010, compact disc.

we pay attention to them? Don't they help us become better teachers? Isn't that part of what it means to be a healthy and mature person? These are good questions, and they have simple answers. Of course other people's perceptions of us matter, and we should try to be aware of them. Of course we need people to encourage us. Affirmation gives us strength, especially when it comes from people we respect and admire. And we also need constructive criticism. Since we are opaque to ourselves, we rely on the counsel of others who see us more clearly than we see ourselves. That is all true, but it is also true that everyone already knows that, and God did not become human to say things everyone already knows. In passages like the one above, Jesus is diagnosing something else, something deeper. He is describing a cycle in which we move beyond a healthy concern for our reputation and become a slave to it, one where we continually put ourselves on display and allow our reputation to dictate our attention—to direct the decisions we make and guide how we move through our days. That is what Barth is warning us against, and he is doing so because he knows that becoming addicted to attention and approval makes the gospel less plausible to the people who hear us talk about it.

Witness

Let's approach the same material from a slightly different angle. When God reveals himself to someone, when he interrupts and awakens someone to his love, he calls that person to become a witness to his love, and Christian existence is "existence in the execution of this task."[16] United to Christ in faith, Christians do not merely receive from him; they also partner with him in the work he is doing in the world. That is the wider theological context in which our teaching is located. When effective, our instruction participates in Jesus Christ's own prophetic self-communication. Intrinsically incapable of making God known, human speech is nevertheless graciously enlisted by God for that purpose. But it would be sheer fantasy to assume that teaching is merely a matter of saying the right words, as if what we say and who we are can somehow be separated from each other. No matter how objectively true our claims about God happen to be, we cannot escape the fact that *we* are the ones making those claims, and the movement of our lives, whether toward or away from the truth, affects how plausible those claims will sound to students. There is no getting

16. CD 4.3.2:575.

around this. If our lives do not somehow witness to the truth, somehow reflect and attest the truth in our own limited ways, students will not find us credible, no matter how impressive our theological reasoning happens to be. In the classroom, we are never *not* teaching. Everything we say and do (and do not do) communicates something to students. An unguarded and revealing casual aside can falsify an entire lecture, indeed an entire semester.

Søren Kierkegaard is relentless on this point. No matter how informed, articulate, and engaging someone happens to be, "it is actual existence that preaches."[17] In other words, your life is your final answer to the question of who you think God is. And there is no good reason to hope students will be persuaded by what you say if, when they examine your life, they conclude that you do not believe what you say. That is precisely why authentic "Christianity has wanted to protect itself against acquiring characterless assistant professors instead of witnesses."[18] Surely we cannot expect

17. Søren Kierkegaard, *For Self-Examination and Judge for Yourself!*, ed. and trans. Howard V. Hong and Edna H. Hong (Princeton: Princeton University Press, 1990).

18. Søren Kierkegaard, *The Moment and Late Writings*, ed. and trans. Howard V. Hong and Edna H. Hong (Princeton: Princeton University Press, 1998), 4. See also his comment, "What we call a teacher in Christianity (pastor) no more resembles what the New Testament understands

students to admire the "vast palace" of our systematic doctrine if they see us living "next door in a barn."[19] Barth expresses this point vividly in a passage Kierkegaard would have loved:

> Only on the lips of someone who is himself affected, seized and committed, controlled and nourished, unsettled and settled, comforted and alarmed by it, can the intrinsically true witness of the act and revelation of God in Jesus Christ have the ring and authority of truth which applies to other people. . . . It can be accepted or even understood only to the extent that he himself has accepted as well as understood what he attests, that he can attest it in his own faith, knowledge and experience as one who has himself been overcome, subdued and determined by it, so that it has taken and continually takes form in his inner and outer life. He cannot, then, be satisfied merely to confess the act and revelation of God as objective truth, and to declare them as such in his speech and conduct. He should naturally do this. But he must show that they are objective truth by attesting them as

---

by a teacher of Christianity than a chest of drawers resembles a dancer, has no more connection with what the New Testament understands as a teacher's task than a chest of drawers has with dancing" (Kierkegaard, *Moment*, 52–53).

19. *KJN* 2:279.

one in whose subjectivity they prove their superiority and in whose humanity they find a reflection and impress. . . . However else it may be with him, less than his own person is not enough if his witness is to be declared as true by him, if it is not to be on his lips as sounding brass or a tinkling symbol, and if therefore, in spite of its truth, it is not to be futile and even false witness with which he dishonors rather than honors his Lord, neither serving him nor helping but only hindering the world and other people. He cannot be a herald to others and himself a castaway.[20]

The longer one ponders this paragraph, the harder it is to imagine a more existentially demanding pedagogical standard. Our theological credibility depends on whether the truth "continually takes form in one's inner and outer life." Only when that happens does our speech have "the ring of truth."

An especially persistent threat to our credibility is what one writer has called a "deadening familiarity with the sublime."[21] Over time, teachers tend to lose touch with the subject matter. Theological speech, once infused with an awareness of God's sheer presence,

20. *CD* 4.3.2:657–58, rev.
21. J. H. Jowett, *The Preacher: His Life and Work* (New York: Hodder & Stoughton, 1912), 44.

withers into abstraction. We begin to relate to Christian theology as if it were a series of puzzles to be solved, claims to be refined, and debates to be adjudicated. The subject matter, once alarmingly close to us, recedes into the distance. Our words, estranged from the reality to which they were meant to point, take on an independent life of their own, and eventually our familiarity with doctrine breeds a kind of spiritual boredom. The God who was once for us a matter of life and death becomes our professional responsibility, our daily routine. As this happens, our students sense it and are instructed by it. As we grow more comfortable in our roles, as we settle into our jobs, as our work becomes more "professional," our teaching often becomes disconnected from its living center in God himself, and the atmosphere of our classes takes on an element of unreality. We manufacture a dreamlike realm in which we move freely, easily, and impressively, naturally assuming the role of expert among amateurs. Gripped by this illusion, we learn to ignore the simple, harrowing fact that we are trying to talk about God.

Consider, for example, how easily we forget that every Christian leader profits off of Jesus Christ's suffering and death. He gets crucified and we get paid. That's the arrangement. Jesus suffers and we cash in. If you teach the Christian faith and that does not unsettle you, you are not thinking straight. None of this is meant to embarrass or immobilize us. Teachers rest in the awareness that God reveals his perfect love through imperfect instruments. But only wishful thinking or willful blindness would lead us to imagine that the plausibility of our speech is unconditioned by the quality of our lives. And while integrity manifests itself differently from person to person, I would like to mention just a few attributes that credible teachers seem to share in common.

Pedagogical Credibility

First, credible teachers sound like themselves. If you pretend to be someone you're not, your students will know.[22] Most students have finely tuned radar for this. They can spot a poser. But sounding like yourself is far more difficult and painful than it sounds. "Of all deceivers, fear yourself most!" Kierkegaard warns.[23] To become honest, to tell the truth, to teach

22. Of course we learn from the example of other teachers. But learning from other teachers—attempting to avoid their weaknesses and assimilate their strengths in our own unique ways—is different from impersonation, which lazily refuses the creative process of authentic assimilation.

23. Kierkegaard, *Moment*, 297.

in your own voice, is not merely a choice you make. It requires an ascetic impulse to examine and acknowledge our weaknesses and insecurities, the vast gaps in our knowledge, the specific defects of our character, and especially the ways our frailties apply pressure on us to compensate for them by manufacturing false personas.[24] Ironically, learning to point away from oneself to Jesus Christ requires sustained self-examination.

Second, credible teachers are aware of the limitations of their vision. While the truth is not relative, our perception of the truth is, and consciousness of our relativity is essential to our credibility. If students see no trace of this awareness in us, if they never detect a hint of hesitation in our voices, never see us struggle with difficult passages or revise our opinions in light of new evidence, can we blame them if they conclude that Christian theology is an intellectualized form of religious propaganda? When they see us condemn one another from positions of assured superiority, all the

24. To be very clear, the impulse I am describing must be sharply distinguished from the faux piety and veiled narcissism of leaders who are forever broadcasting their weaknesses in public to earn praise from their audiences. Additionally, it is true that honesty often requires us to act against our impulses and inclinations, to do the opposite of what comes naturally to us, but that's not what I'm talking about here.

while appealing to the same Scriptures, are they wrong to be unimpressed? Should we be surprised if they remain skeptical about our testimony concerning God's love in Christ when they watch us mercilessly devour anyone who strays from the party line? Once students realize how easy it is to play the "endless game" of demonstrating that "we members of this group are right for precisely this or that reason, and everyone else is wrong," many of them lose interest in Christian theology as a whole.[25] The absurdity of our parochial certainties becomes too much for them. Obviously it is a mistake for students to dismiss the discipline because it can be practiced badly, but that is not the point. The question is whether that decision is plausible in light of the evidence we provide them. And it will be, unless we teach with a sober recognition of our own fallibility and the fallibility of the traditions to which we belong.

Third, credible teachers are willing to undermine their own authority. If our vision is limited, so too is our authority. Our teaching is authoritative only to the extent that we tell the truth about God. God alone possesses intrinsic theological authority. He is

25. Karl Barth, *The Word of God and Theology*, trans. Amy Marga (London: T&T Clark, 2011), 24–25, rev.

the norm of every theological statement. Moreover, Holy Scripture, the ecumenical creeds and definitions, and the confessions of our particular traditions all carry more weight than the opinions of any single theologian. But it's not enough to agree with these claims theoretically. We have to communicate them to students—directly perhaps, but more often indirectly, through the kind of relationships we adopt to the subject matter and to them. Ironically, the more persuasive we are, the more likely students will be to repeat what we say rather than to learn to think for themselves. When a difficult question arises, many students will instinctively look to us to supply the answer. Good teachers are aware of this and continually attempt to help students break this habit. When a theologian of the stature of Karl Barth makes statements such as the following, that is precisely what he is doing: "The angels laugh at old Karl. They laugh at him because he tries to grasp the truth about God in a book of *Dogmatics*. They laugh at the fact that volume follows volume and each is thicker than the previous one. As they laugh, they say to one another, 'Look! Here he comes now with his little pushcart full of volumes of the *Dogmatics*!'—and they laugh about the people who write so much about Karl Barth instead of writing about the things he is trying to write about. Truly, the angels laugh."[26]

Of course adopting this attitude is easier said than done, and perhaps easiest for someone like Barth, who received so much praise. The rest of us, under various kinds of pressure to make a name for ourselves, face the strong temptation to inflate our importance, emphasize our indispensability, and communicate a general air of knowing superiority. Yet this is all a pointless waste of time. Not only because academic glory is fickle and fleeting, or even because self-important theologians are just embarrassing and sad, but also and primarily because snobbery and self-promotion make us less persuasive witnesses. They turn us into teachers who specialize in drawing attention to ourselves rather than teachers who aspire to disappear in front of a room full of students captivated by the subject matter.

To illustrate this point, and to sum up this chapter, I'd like to end with a story about Andrés Iniesta, the best Spanish soccer player of all time. Iniesta is a

26. Quoted in George Casalis, *Portrait of Karl Barth* (Garden City, NY: Doubleday, 1963), 3. See also Barth's comment, "It is curious still to be so much a beginner at the age of seventy three" (quoted in Eberhard Busch, *The Great Passion: An Introduction to Karl Barth's Theology*, ed. Darrell L. Guder and Judith Guder, trans. Geoffrey W. Bromiley [Grand Rapids: Eerdmans, 2004], 441).

genius. He's as good at what he does as almost anyone in any field of endeavor. He's tiny—five-foot-seven, 140 pounds, with legs so skinny you half expect them to break every time he gets tackled. But after the Champions League Final in 2009, Wayne Rooney, the most well-known British player other than David Beckham, said Iniesta was the best player in the world, better even than Lionel Messi, who many people think is the greatest player in *history*. The point is that Iniesta is really, really good, and because of that he has every reason to be a preening megalomaniac, a narcissist like Cristiano Ronaldo. But he's not. In fact, he is exactly the opposite. Once, he was in a Barcelona restaurant and a waitress who thought he was the busboy ordered him to clear a table full of dirty dishes—and he did, without missing a beat. Anyway, in 2010 Spain and Holland met in the World Cup final and played to a scoreless draw. Then in the 116th minute of extra time, Iniesta drifted wide, received a pass, and with a lunging Dutch defender closing in on him, rifled a shot past the goalkeeper and into the net. With that one act, Iniesta won Spain its first World Cup and sent an entire nation into collective ecstasy. No one in sports history has ever been higher than Iniesta was at that moment. He had reached the summit of individual sporting achievement. And then, with more than a billion people watching him, and with a significant percentage of those people worshiping him, he ripped off his jersey in celebration and revealed his undershirt, shown in the picture below. It says, "Dani Jarque siempre con nosotros"—"Dani Jarque always with us." It's a tribute to a friend and former teammate who died the year before of a heart attack.

Martin Meissner/AP/Corbis

So think for a second about what you're looking at here. A man prepares his entire life for this moment, and when it finally arrives he manages to hold his nerve and seize it. And with the eyes of 15 percent of the world's population fixed on him, what does he do next? He directs all the glory and attention away from himself to someone else. He becomes less so that someone else can become greater. He becomes invisible so that someone else can become visible. It's hard to imagine a more vivid parable of self-emptying Christian existence than that. In that one gesture, Iniesta showed us what it looks like for someone to disappear in front of a billion people. And in the slightly less stratospheric contexts of our classrooms, let us pray that God will extend us the grace to do the same.

4

DANGER

Today we hear a lot about the need for students to feel safe in our classrooms. This makes a certain amount of sense. If students experience a class as demeaning, if they aren't confident their questions, experiences, and ideas are being taken seriously, if they decide a teacher doesn't particularly care about them as human beings, or if they sense they're being coerced or manipulated, they probably aren't going to learn much. Few of us open ourselves to people we think are hostile or indifferent toward us. But it's also true that if students feel only affirmed in our classes, if our classes never disturb, unsettle, or expose them, if they never find themselves fighting for their lives, then they probably aren't going to learn much in that kind of environment either.

This is especially true when teaching Christianity. The atmosphere of our classes ought to cohere as much as possible with the reality we are attempting to describe. And since Christian theology occurs as an encounter with the living God, a confrontation that tears us away from patterns of life that obscure or contradict the truth, at least something of the spirit of that struggle ought to be reflected in our classrooms. If Isaiah's response is paradigmatic of every serious confrontation with God—"Woe is me!"—and if it is impossible to "withdraw more or less unscathed from the shock that makes one a theologian," then the last thing teachers ought to do is shelter students from the life-giving trauma of this encounter.[1]

In an utterly non-coercive way—in a way that respects students' freedom, affords them space to explore the mysteries of the faith, encourages them to draw their own conclusions, and eschews every kind of manipulation and indoctrination—we have to make it clear to students that the subject matter of Christian theology demands a decision, and it demands a decision now. Notice, the subject matter demands a decision—not the teacher! *The Word* cries

1. *ET*, 116.

out for belief, for acceptance in recognition, trust, and obedience."[2] Careful description, probing interrogation, incisive criticism, and broad cataloging of options play an important role when Christianity is taught well, but we mislead students unless we clarify that Jesus Christ, *as the New Testament describes him*, is someone whose life demands a personal response. As Karl Barth puts it: "Any theology which would not even consider the necessity to respond to God personally could only be false theology."[3] Søren Kierkegaard expresses this point in a vivid analogy:

> We all know what it is to play at war, that it is to *simulate* as convincingly as possible everything that happens in war: the troops line up, they take the field, everyone looks serious but also full of courage and enthusiasm, the orderlies dash back and forth fearlessly, the officers' voices are heard, the signals, the battle cries, the musket volleys, the thunder of cannon . . . everything, everything just as in war; only one thing is lacking—the dangers. So it is with playing at Christianity—it is to simulate the Christian proclamation in such a way that everything, everything, everything is included as convincingly as possible, but one thing is

2. *ET*, 37. Emphasis added.
3. *ET*, 165.

omitted—the dangers. In the proclamation as it is in the New Testament, the whole emphasis falls on the personal—this accounts for the dangers; when we play at Christianity, the thing to do (but carefully, convincingly) is to draw attention away from the personal—so the dangers are also absent.[4]

And yet, despite appearances, when you're standing in front of a group of students, you cannot reliably discern if the battle you see taking place in front of you is real. Because what looks and feels like a real fight might actually be a pseudo struggle, where nothing is at stake and nothing important is happening; and what appears to be a lull in the action, a minor skirmish, or even a truce, may in fact be lethal combat for a student. You just can't tell. Teachers are incapable of measuring and assessing the work God is (or is not) doing in the classroom.[5] And strangely enough, one of the easiest ways to misread the situation is to be misled when students tell you how much they enjoy

4. Søren Kierkegaard, *The Moment and Late Writings*, ed. and trans. Howard V. Hong and Edna H. Hong (Princeton: Princeton University Press, 1998), 433.

5. Despite the prevailing methodological assumptions that govern American education today, many important elements of education cannot be measured or assessed, and in the case of Christian theology, that is true about the most important elements.

your classes. To be sure, if students hate your classes, it's probably your fault, and your teaching needs to change. But if students like your classes, if they are attentive and engaged, if you get almost exclusively positive feedback on your course evaluations, and if students routinely praise your teaching, it's nearly impossible not to draw the conclusion that your teaching is successful. And yet if students enjoy your classes, it may mean nothing more than that they enjoy your classes. The lasting effect may run no deeper than that. But then, so what? Can you think of anything more inane than a Christian theologian who thinks his or her classes are successful just because everyone likes them and no one feels uncomfortable?

And the same thing is true from the opposite side. Students are easily tricked into thinking a class worked just because they enjoyed it. I've taught whole courses on Christology where I've said all sorts of things except the one thing students most need to hear. Yet they came to class and enjoyed the experience. They read the books, wrote the papers, and never noticed that I neglected to raise the question that Jesus himself continually asks each one of us: "Okay fine, but who do *you* say that I am?" Still, at the end of the semester, most of them gave five stars and wrote encouraging notes in the comment boxes. But what they should have done, and maybe what they would have done if they had realized what was happening, is criticize me for engineering a class that was perfectly safe for them and, I now realize, even safer for me.

Of course, if you could pick your problems, this is the one you'd pick. Because while a useless class can pulse with energy and tension, we all know that ineffective classes can also become soul-wearingly boring for students. We care about the material and expect students to care too. Nevertheless, many of them remain uninterested, and we can't figure out why. At our worst, we become frustrated and curmudgeonly and start complaining about how incurious students are these days, and how they're not serious enough, and how they're distracted by trivia and technology, and how we wish they were smarter, and whatever else we feel like complaining about. But there's usually a much simpler reason why we bore them. We bore them because we're boring.

And very often, even when students are mildly interested, what we teach them remains detached and sealed in some ethereal and abstract theologico-academic realm that hovers above them, without making meaningful contact with the daily rhythms and concerns of their

lives. They struggle to see what difference our courses
make for ordinary life and ministry. And the really un-
forgivable thing is how little time we spend helping them
imagine these connections. Maybe we even have some
convoluted rationale for why doing so is not our responsibility. We operate as though training students to
trace the repercussions of the material into their lives is
ancillary to our important work—if we think it is part
of our work at all. But in addition to describing and
examining theological ideas, a fully Christian approach
to teaching Christian theology will involve helping students perceive some of the concrete implications of the
material, and thus help them live less divided lives.

Maybe it's like this. If you were in the mood to listen,
I could tell you all about the underlying and evolving
tactical philosophy that animates the way FC Barcelona plays soccer: their eccentric approach to time and
space, the way players interchange positions, how they
defend while possessing the ball, and so on. And you
might find what I had to say interesting, even intellectually exciting in its own way. But no matter how
fascinating you found the ideas, it would never occur
to you that any of it pertained to you personally, and
it would never occur to me to talk to you as if it did.
But now imagine you're Andrés Iniesta, and you've

been at the club since you were a boy, and you're on the training ground before an important match, and the manager is explaining the team's tactics. In that case, you would hear everything differently. The tactical philosophy would acquire new meaning, since you would listen as an insider rather than an outsider, as someone responsible for responding to it rather than merely thinking about it. Similarly, if the reality of God's reconciling love for the world in Christ teaches us anything about our students, anything at all, it teaches us that they are always already insiders to God's grace. Each one of them is at every moment personally addressed by God in Christ. God continually calls them not merely to listen but to act—not merely to reflect on the truth but to become truthful. Indeed, recognition of the truth (who they are in Christ) is inseparable from responsiveness to the truth (becoming who they are in Christ), and helping students perceive this—or perceive it more clearly—is a distinguishing feature of all good teaching.

"Nicodemus Was Dreaming"

The Gospels could hardly be clearer that one cannot know Jesus from a safe distance. Consider, for example, his conversation with Nicodemus. Nicodemus was impressed by Jesus. He could see that Jesus was "a teacher who has come from God" (John 3:2). Moved by Jesus's wisdom and power, Nicodemus wanted to have "a cautious, judicious, tolerant, religious conversation—as from one bank of a stream to another."[6] If there has ever been a sincere religious seeker, it was Nicodemus. He had "real questions, earnest burning questions," and he was perceptive enough to recognize that Jesus could answer them.[7] In fact, Nicodemus's earnestness is precisely what makes Jesus's response to him so shocking. Rather than entering into respectful dialogue with Nicodemus, Jesus immediately launched an attack: "No one can see the kingdom of God without being born from above" (John 3:3). With that one assertion, "all the cards were struck from Nicodemus' hand. All his chartered positions were unrolled before the battle began. He finds himself face to face with something new and incomprehensible, something he cannot fathom."[8] Stunned and confused, Nicodemus mumbled a question about the meaning of old people being born, and when Jesus

6. Karl Barth and Eduard Thurneysen, "Jesus and Nicodemus," in *Come Holy Spirit: Sermons*, trans. George W. Richards, Elmer G. Homrighausen, and Karl J. Ernst (New York: Round Table Press, 1933), 102.

7. Barth and Thurneysen, "Jesus and Nicodemus," 105.

8. Barth and Thurneysen, "Jesus and Nicodemus," 102–3, rev.

confounded him with the further claim that to enter the kingdom of God one has to be born of water and the Spirit, he weakly muttered, "How can these things be?" (John 3:9). To which Jesus ironically replied, "Are you a teacher of Israel, and yet you do not understand these things?" (John 3:10). And just like that, "Nicodemus was check-mated by three moves."[9]

Notice what's happening here. Nicodemus wanted to engage Jesus in serious religious discussion—the kind of careful and sincere dialogue that takes place between two generous and informed conversation partners exchanging opinions with each other. But Nicodemus managed only a single confident sentence before Jesus overwhelmed and silenced him. "Nicodemus must have felt as if suddenly a flashing sword was swung over him while he sat there with harmless and friendly intent."[10] And as readers, we find ourselves disoriented right along with him. What did Nicodemus do to receive such rough treatment? Why would Jesus attack someone seeking earnest conversation? Was it really necessary to speak to Nicodemus so sharply and abrasively?

9. Barth and Thurneysen, "Jesus and Nicodemus," 103. Cf. Mike Tyson's Rule: "Everybody has a plan until they get punched in the mouth."
10. Barth and Thurneysen, "Jesus and Nicodemus," 107.

The longer you ponder these questions, the clearer the answers become. Jesus wanted Nicodemus to see the truth, but he could tell that "Nicodemus was dreaming."[11] He recognized that Nicodemus had no idea who he was talking to and did not perceive how dangerous discussing God really is. So to open his eyes, Jesus needed to shatter Nicodemus's illusions. To heal him, Jesus had to wound him. Or to change the metaphor, "Jesus saw Nicodemus standing, as it were, under a roof that kept him from looking toward heaven. He could not show him heaven at all, as long as he was under the roof, even though he would have taken endless pains to do so. Therefore he did the only thing that he could do. He tried from the first to take him away from the roof and lead him under the open heavens, to place him upon wholly new ground."[12] Seen in this light, what initially appears as an unnecessary assault turns out to be an act of divine kindness. Jesus's apparent refusal to listen to Nicodemus is in fact an event of profound empathy. Jesus understood Nicodemus better than Nicodemus understood himself. Nicodemus was oblivious to what was really happening. He thought he was seeking Jesus, but the reader perceives

11. Barth and Thurneysen, "Jesus and Nicodemus," 109.
12. Barth and Thurneysen, "Jesus and Nicodemus," 109.

(and perhaps Nicodemus eventually did too) that Jesus was seeking Nicodemus—seeking, that is, to awaken Nicodemus to reality. Had Jesus allowed Nicodemus to converse with him from a safe distance, converse with him on Nicodemus's own terms, Nicodemus's illusion would only have been reinforced. Thus Jesus needed to give him "a sharp jolt."[13]

We see this kind of encounter throughout the Gospels. Conversations with Jesus rarely unfold according to plan. Jesus continually shocks and astonishes people, rattles their cages, upends their expectations, eludes their traps, and zeroes in on their deepest motivations. This makes for exhilarating reading, but the more you reflect on it, the more unsettling it becomes. As you watch Jesus stride through the narrative, you begin to realize that being near him requires courage. It dawns on you that if you are afraid of the truth, afraid of being exposed, you better keep your distance. And even when you do manage to screw up the courage to move closer to Jesus, to open yourself to him earnestly and sincerely, you never know what will happen next. Jesus is beyond predicting. To be clear, God's love for us in Christ is absolutely secure and

13. Barth and Thurneysen, "Jesus and Nicodemus," 109.

dependable, and knowing this is essential for teaching and studying Christian theology well. Without this confidence, theological inquiry would be an exercise in anxiety. As Kierkegaard saw so clearly, "love gives unbounded courage"—exactly the kind of courage that theological study requires.[14] But the constancy of divine love does not manifest itself in a stable, cozy relationship. In fact, just the opposite. According to the New Testament, following Jesus is as precarious as it is unpredictable. In a sermon ostensibly about Jeremiah, but expressing his own agonizing experience of discipleship, Dietrich Bonhoeffer writes,

> O Lord, you have enticed me, and I was enticed. I had no idea what was coming when you seized me—and now I cannot get away from you anymore; you have carried me off as your booty. You tie us to your victory chariot and pull us along behind you. . . . How could we know that your love hurts so much; that your grace is so stern? . . . You have bound me to you for better or worse. God, why are you so terrifyingly near to us? . . . God, why are you so close to us? Not to be able to get away from God is the constant disquieting thing in the

14. Søren Kierkegaard, *Eighteen Upbuilding Discourses*, ed. and trans. Howard V. Hong and Edna H. Hong (Princeton: Princeton University Press, 1990), 65.

life of every Christian. If once you let God into your life, if you once allow yourself to be enticed by God, you will never get away again—as a child never gets away from its mother, as a man never gets away from the woman whom he loves.[15]

This passage is arresting not because Bonhoeffer is describing an uncommon experience but because he gives voice to what it feels like to attach yourself to a God who is completely beyond your control. Bonhoeffer is describing an experience that many Christians have but few manage to express with such honesty and eloquence—namely, that following Jesus hurts, and that becoming his disciple means "entering into endless insecurity."[16] One of the most striking features of the Gospels is how they make no attempt to hide any of this. Anyone who reads the New Testament and who attempts to follow Jesus according to the pattern of life described there knows that when Jesus enters the comfortable living room of your life, he throws the furniture around.[17] He leads you to places

15. *DBWE* 13:351–52.
16. *DBWE* 4:62.
17. Stealing Flannery O'Connor's imagery. See her comment, "I distrust folks who have ugly things to say about Karl Barth. I like old Barth. He throws the furniture around" (quoted in Ralph C. Wood, *Flannery*

you don't want to go. He lays waste to the fortresses you construct to protect yourself against his love. "To believe in Jesus is the most hazardous of all hazards,"[18] Barth writes, and Kierkegaard agrees: "In the New Testament, Christianity is the deepest wound that can be inflicted upon a person. It is calculated to collide on the most terrifying scale with everything."[19]

The Opposite of Good Teaching

Before moving on, allow me to clarify the blindingly obvious. I am describing the Christian life, the risks and perils inherent in following Jesus. I am emphatically not recommending that teachers assume an analogously disruptive role in the classroom. To misunderstand this point would inevitably lead to misery for teacher and student alike. Consider, for example, a teacher who makes it his personal mission to unsettle and attack the supposedly naive and benighted faith of his students. Convinced of the superiority of his wisdom and the righteousness of his cause, he seeks

---

O'Connor and the Christ-Haunted South [Grand Rapids: Eerdmans, 2004], 10).

   18. Karl Barth, *The Epistle to the Romans*, trans. Edwyn C. Hoskyns (Oxford: Oxford University Press, 1968), 99.

   19. *KJN* 9:313.

to dismantle and destroy untutored devotion wherever he encounters it. Such a person is as confused as he is contemptible. Instead of teaching, it would be better if he tied a stone around his neck and threw himself into the sea (Luke 17:2). Teaching Christianity is an act of love. Teachers are called to help students perceive and respond to the truth, not to threaten, provoke, or scandalize them. That almost goes without saying. And yet it should be similarly obvious, at least to anyone who has read the New Testament, that to describe Christianity responsibly requires honesty about what knowing God and following Christ are really like.

Divine Presence

Given the sheer quantity of disruptive and disorienting encounters people have with Jesus in the New Testament, I doubt many teachers would explicitly argue against the harrowing descriptions of discipleship we find in Kierkegaard, Barth, and Bonhoeffer. The greater temptation is to minimize or ignore this dimension of Christian existence. When we make this mistake, we do so in countless ways and for reasons too numerous to list or explore here, but one form of this error seems especially common and insidious:

we tend to talk about God as if he is not present. Few things are harder than remembering that God is alive and active in our classrooms, few things easier than teaching as if he is not. Imagine you and I are having a conversation about someone. Whatever we happen to be saying about that person, no matter how positive or negative our comments happen to be, the conversation will shift if that person suddenly walks into the room. Her presence with us will change the atmosphere of our discussion. We will stop talking one way and start talking another way. The same is true about God. If we think he is present in our classrooms, that will affect how we talk about him, and if we don't think he is present (or forget that he is), that will too. In other words, we instruct students not only by *what* we say about God but also by *how* we speak about him.

This leads us back to the themes of the previous chapter. If our way of talking about God leaves students unaware of the threat he poses to our lives, perhaps that is because we no longer perceive the threat he poses to our lives. This is an abiding occupational hazard of everyone who teaches Christian theology. As we become more professionally competent, more familiar with the history of theology, more assured in our knowledge and clear about our commitments, we easily assume an air of knowingness, an attitude of self-assured security that exudes confidence and control. As we become comfortable in our role as experts on the topic of God, professionals with theological answers at our fingertips, this attitude manifests itself in our teaching, and students are instructed by it. The clarity of Kierkegaard's perception of this point is invaluable.

> In general there are two decisive errors with respect to Christianity. First, Christianity is not a doctrine but an existence-communication. This is the source of all the nuisances of orthodoxy, its quarrels about one thing and another, while existence remains totally unchanged, so that people quarrel about what is Christian just as they do about what is Platonic philosophy and the like. . . . Second, consequently (because Christianity is not a doctrine) in relation to it, it is not a matter of indifference who presents it, as with a doctrine, provided only that he (objectively) says the right thing.—No, Christ appointed not assistant professors—but followers. If Christianity, precisely because it is not a doctrine, does not reduplicate itself in the person who presents it, then what he is presenting is not Christianity. For Christianity is an existence-communication and can only

be presented—by existing. Fundamentally, to exist in it is of course to express it in existence, etc.—it is to reduplicate.[20]

For all his emphasis on the freedom of God's self-communication, the frailty and fallibility of God's human witnesses, the non-contingency of the truth upon those called to articulate it, and the abiding sinfulness and self-deception of even the holiest among us, Barth, dogmatic theologian par excellence, agreed with Kierkegaard that Christianity cannot be reduced to doctrines about God and that Christian existence conditions the plausibility of Christian speech.[21] And if they are right, then either our teaching—including who we are, the ways we speak about God, and the atmosphere we cultivate in our classes—will suggest God's urgent uncontrollable presence with us, his "terrifying nearness" as Bonhoeffer put it, or our teaching will mislead students. There are no exceptions to this rule.

20. *KJN* 5:39, rev.

21. See Barth's comment, "It is good and right to point to the significance of the individual personality of the instructor. In the last analysis, it is the case that the mystery of instruction and of research lies in the person" (Karl Barth, *Barth in Conversation*, ed. Eberhard Busch, trans. The Translation Fellows of the Center for Barth Studies Princeton Theological Seminary, vol. 1, *1959–1962* [Louisville: Westminster John Knox, 2017], 67).

Safety

But this kind of teaching is way easier said than done—not only because attending to the presence of God and losing the illusion of control require more spiritual discipline and maturity than most of us possess, and not even because such teaching is an expression of the orientation of one's whole life rather than a pedagogical technique one can master, but also because many students do not want this kind of teaching. Some do—or at least they welcome it when they encounter it—but many students enter our classes seeking various forms of safety, security, and control. They want a teacher who will offer them sanctuary from the various threats inherent to Christian existence, someone who will alleviate the difficulty by reducing some of the risks associated with believing in God. This desire takes many forms, but two seem especially common.

The first is a search for the security of theological certainty. Whether confused by the chaos of contemporary life, caught in patterns of doubt, threatened by the existence of intelligent unbelievers, unnerved by the complexity and diversity of the church's own history of theological reflection, or for countless other reasons, many students seek refuge in a teacher who will tell them what to think. They want an expert who will provide them with definitive theological solutions, someone who will tie up the loose ends and alleviate the various pressures they are experiencing. The last thing these students want is a teacher who requires them to make their own theological decisions—a teacher through whom they come to realize that Christianity is even more demanding than they realized.

For other students, the desire for security takes the mirror-opposite form. Rather than unreservedly committing themselves to a single teacher or tradition, they embrace the safety of ceaseless uncertainty. For these students, theological education becomes a process of endless deliberation. Forever reading, thinking, and talking, they never get around to making decisions. Theological reflection and conversation become substitutes for theological commitment. Protected by the fact that there is always more to learn, another angle to consider, a new position to evaluate, these students retreat into a state of permanently suspended judgment in which they are "always being instructed and can never arrive at a knowledge of the truth" (2 Tim. 3:7). While superficially different, these two outlooks share a common unwillingness to embrace the risks associated with Christian existence.

To the second group of students, those stuck in the cycle of endless deliberation, Kierkegaard makes the telling observation that delay is itself a decision: "A person indeed *must* choose—God is not mocked. Thus it is truly the case that if a person avoids choosing, this is the same as the blasphemy of choosing the world."[22] Since rational deliberation is open-ended, there will always be reasons—often very good reasons—to postpone making a definite theological commitment. But permanent postponement is indistinguishable from unbelief. Moreover, no amount of additional contemplation will lead these students out of the cycle of perpetual analysis. For that to happen, something else is required.

> If someone wanted to be [Christ's] follower, [Christ's] approach, as seen in the Gospel, was different from lecturing. To such a person he said something like this: Venture a decisive act; then we can begin. What does this mean? It means that one does not become a Christian by hearing something about Christianity, by reading something about it, by thinking about it, or, while Christ was living, by seeing him once in a while or by going and staring at him all day long. No,

22. Kierkegaard, *Eighteen Upbuilding Discourses*, 207.

a setting (a situation) is required—venture a decisive act; the proof does not precede but follows, is in and with the imitation that follows Christ.[23]

As he so often does, Bonhoeffer agrees with Kierke-gaard here: "You see, there are always reasons not to do something; the question is whether you do it in spite of them. If you only want to do things that have every reason in their favor, you'll end up never doing anything, or else it won't be necessary any longer, since others will have taken over for you. Yet every real deed is one that no one else can do, only you yourself."[24]

The first group of students, those seeking to submit to an authoritative teacher, demonstrate an analo-gous unwillingness to step into the fray. Rather than engaging in the struggle of real theological educa-tion, these students expect their teachers to do the hard work for them.[25] And yet, since secondhand knowledge of God is impossible, since God is always

23. Søren Kierkegaard, *For Self-Examination and Judge for Yourself!*, ed. and trans. Howard V. Hong and Edna H. Hong (Princeton: Princeton University Press, 1990), 191.

24. *DBWE* 8:425.

25. As Kierkegaard once observed, "There are many people who arrive at answers in life just like schoolboys; they cheat their teacher by copying the answer out of the arithmetic book without having worked the problem out themselves" (*KJN* 2:75).

known in the context of a living relationship that never passes over into human control, since theological knowledge cannot be reduced to pieces of intellectual data that teachers accumulate, organize, and dispense, teachers are incapable of offering these students what they want. We cannot give them what we do not possess. Real theological education is a process of continual confrontation with God. To receive it, students have to fight for it themselves. The most teachers can do is participate in this apprenticeship alongside them.

> Is truth such that in relation to it one may suppose that a person can appropriate it summarily with the help of another? Summarily, that is, without willing oneself to be developed in like manner, to be tried, to battle, to suffer as did the one who acquired the truth for him? Is it not just as impossible as to sleep or dream oneself into the truth; is it not just as impossible summarily to appropriate it, however wide awake one is? Or if one is wide awake, is it not merely an illusion if one does not understand or refuses to understand that in relation to truth there is no abridgment that leaves out the acquiring of it, and that in relation to acquiring it from generation to generation there is no essential abridgment, so that every generation

and everyone in the generation must essentially begin from the beginning?[26]

Students unwilling to enter *and remain* in this struggle can obviously read and understand Scripture and Christian theology, but true knowledge of God involves the whole person, not merely the intellect. In Kierkegaard's unforgettable formulation, "The truth is a trap: you cannot get hold of it without getting caught; you cannot get hold of the truth in such a way that you catch it, but only in such a way that it catches you."[27] Thus the rhythm of revelation is continual renewal. The God whom Christian theology seeks to know "again and again discloses himself anew and must be discovered anew."[28] Rather than becoming the believer's permanent possession, knowledge of God is "constantly being acquired."[29] Barth draws the inevitable conclusion that follows from this line of reasoning—an inference that I suspect will sound odd to many people who sign up for Christian theology

26. Søren Kierkegaard, *Practice in Christianity*, ed. and trans. Howard V. Hong and Edna H. Hong (Princeton: Princeton University Press, 1991), 202–3.

27. *KJN* 10:17.

28. *ET*, 6.

29. Kierkegaard, *Eighteen Upbuilding Discourses*, 14.

classes: "We cannot, therefore, define Christians simply as those who are awake while the rest sleep, but more cautiously as those who wake up in the sense that they are awakened a first time and then again and again. . . . They are, in fact, those who constantly stand in need of reawakening and who depend upon the fact that they are continually reawakened. They are thus those who, it is to be hoped, continually wake up."[30]

The Price of Real Education

Throughout this chapter I have stressed that real knowledge of God happens for only those students willing to embrace the risks it involves. If I am right about that, then theological education is not something teachers can give students, nor is it something students can buy. What students pay for is entrance into a context in which they *might* be educated, and that happens only for those courageous, assiduous, and vulnerable enough to enter the perilous process of continual reawakening that Barth describes. But real education is as demanding for teachers as it is for students. Responsible teaching requires honesty.

30. *CD* 4.2:555.

It requires teachers to clarify the dangers inherent in Christian existence and to cultivate classroom environments that suggest those difficulties. But the costs associated with such teaching are rapidly increasing. As educational institutions compete for students like businesses compete for customers, as university campuses are transformed into "retirement spreads for the young," as student evaluations factor heavily in assessment and promotion decisions, and as the very idea of liberal education rapidly loses ground to utilitarian strategies for career training, teachers face extraordinary pressure to pander to students and downplay the requirements of serious education.[31] And what is true in academia is likewise true in the church. Pastors and teachers are pressed on all sides to make "everything as convenient, as comfortable and as inexpensive as possible."[32] The pressure to sell Christianity at discount prices is intense, and Christian leaders who refuse to adjust to these conditions create very real problems for themselves. I would not presume to advise anyone negotiating these challenges, nor do I claim to have navigated them well myself. I have made

31. Mark Edmundson, *Why Teach? In Defense of a Real Education* (New York: Bloomsbury, 2013), ix.

32. Kierkegaard, *Moment*, 109.

numerous concessions along the way and do not claim to be an example of truly courageous teaching. I have never reached the end of a semester and been pleased with my performance. Not once. I consider myself guilty of what Kierkegaard called "playing at Christianity and making a fool of God."[33] The most I can say for myself is that I am trying to learn to teach courses that cohere more closely with the reality I am attempting to describe. And since I see no reason to hope that abstract and undemanding courses will faithfully communicate the truth about knowing God and following Christ, I plan to keep trying.

33. Kierkegaard, *Moment*, 168, rev.

5

CONVERSATION

God is talkative, and our communion with him is conversational.[1] Instead of concealing himself in silence or declaring himself from a distance, God speaks the world into existence and strikes up conversation with his creation. He establishes and sustains Israel with words, and in Jesus Christ the words he speaks are his own life. The Logos invites us into dialogue, and Christian faith is the long process of learning to hear and respond to Jesus Christ's voice. Since Christian discipleship and theology are thoroughly conversational, teaching

1. "Long ago God spoke to our ancestors in many and various ways by the prophets, but in these last days he has spoken to us by a Son" (Heb. 1:2). See Robert Jenson, *A Theology in Outline: Can These Bones Live?* (New York: Oxford University Press, 2016).

Christian theology necessarily includes instruction in the art of conversation.

New Challenges

While providing this instruction has never been easy, it has become especially difficult in recent years. Compared to the students I taught when I arrived at Whitworth sixteen years ago, my current students are no less intelligent and dedicated. With very few exceptions, they are receptive and eager to learn. Although their lives are more crowded with technology, and more of them bear the additional weight of anxiety and depression, they are as clever and creative as my former students, and equally invested in their work. They often make significant personal and financial sacrifices to attend college. Reliably earnest and kind, they are playful and attentive, often penetratingly insightful, and rarely condescending or judgmental. I like them, and I like being around them. They are a pleasure to teach. Quite a few have become my close friends. Yet whereas my classes used to be full of people whose default instinct was to participate in lively classroom discussion, most of my current students prefer to listen and observe. Few are temperamentally inclined to engage in vigorous open-ended dialogue. Alert and perceptive, they listen carefully and track arguments well, but most would rather watch conversations unfold than participate in them.

This change has altered the mood of my courses. The classroom *feels* different than it did a decade ago—at least at the beginning of each semester. When my colleagues and I discuss this, we (predictably, I know) speculate about how smartphones and social media seem to be changing students. When so many students tell us their digital lives are out of control, when they confess to being unable to unplug for extended periods of time without symptoms of withdrawal, when class ends and most students reflexively reach for their phones, we suspect this somehow contributes to their diminished appetite for public dialogue. As it turns out, it probably does.

Sherry Turkle has constructed a compelling argument in support of the claim that our misuse of digital media contributes to conversational decline.[2] According to Turkle, smartphones and computers condition us to avoid face-to-face conversation and genuine

2. Sherry Turkle, *Reclaiming Conversation: The Power of Talk in a Digital Age* (New York: Penguin, 2015). Turkle is a sociologist, clinical psychologist, and professor at MIT.

solitude, both of which are necessary for the development of self-reflection, empathy, and other essential
human qualities. Accustomed to a continuous feed
of digitally mediated information and entertainment,
we move away from personal encounters we cannot
control. "Real people, with their unpredictable ways,
can seem difficult to contend with after one has spent
a stretch in simulation."[3] Moreover, this retreat from
others coincides with a retreat from ourselves. Al-
lergic to boredom, craving constant stimulation and
distraction, we eschew the silence and solitude necessary to develop independent reflection and a stable
sense of ourselves. "Afraid of being alone, we struggle
to pay attention to ourselves. And what suffers is our
ability to pay attention to each other. If we can't find
our own center, we lose confidence in what we have
to offer others. Or you can work the circle the other
way: We struggle to pay attention to each other, and
what suffers is our ability to know ourselves. We face
a flight from conversation that is also a flight from
self-reflection, empathy, and mentorship."[4] According
to Turkle, these patterns show up clearly in college
students, whose levels of empathy appear to be 40

3. Turkle, *Reclaiming Conversation*, 7.
4. Turkle, *Reclaiming Conversation*, 10–11.

percent lower than those of students from a couple decades ago, with most of the decline happening in the last decade.[5] It is no surprise, then, that college students are shying away from the kind of probing face-to-face conversations they are increasingly less equipped to have.

Yet for all her clear-eyed analysis of these alarming trends, Turkle mounts an aggressive case against resignation and despair. Despite the trouble we've gotten ourselves into, things change—*we* change—when we put our phones away, talk to one another, and learn to be alone. I am less optimistic than Turkle that this will happen on anything like a broad scale, since so many of the corporations that increasingly dominate our lives have such a massive financial stake in keeping us hooked on our devices.[6] But if Turkle is right about our resilience, if the damage is reversible, if genuine solitude and robust conversation heal and humanize, that is something teachers need to know. Yes, the symptoms are acute, and yes, we have our work cut out for us, but training students in the art of conversation is,

5. According to evidence collated from seventy-two studies; see Turkle, *Reclaiming Conversation*, 21 and 370.

6. See Adam Alter's disturbing *Irresistible: The Rise of Addictive Technology and the Business of Keeping Us Hooked* (New York: Penguin, 2017).

even now, possible and worth the effort. And that is just as well, since teaching Christian theology is largely a matter of training students to have good theological conversations.

Christian Theology: The Primary and Secondary Conversations

Christian theology is a historically extended conversation about the meaning and implications of the gospel. It is thinking and speaking that seeks to respond in disciplined, faithful, and creative ways to God's own self-communication. In what Karl Barth calls the primary conversation of Christian theology, theological students (teachers and pupils alike) inquire directly into Scripture, seeking to hear and respond to the testimony of the prophets and apostles.[7] To learn Christian theology is to be initiated into this conversation: "Ultimately and in its most decisive aspects, today's instruction is but an introduction to the source and norm of all theology: namely, the testimony of Holy Scripture."[8] Hearing "this voice *anew* at every moment," Barth writes, is "the funda-

7. *ET*, 174.
8. *ET*, 173.

mental task of all theological study."[9] But since no one is inspired, clever, or wise enough to engage in this conversation alone, students participate in what Barth calls a secondary conversation in which they receive guidance from fellow students (past and present) engaged in the same work.[10] These two conversations take place simultaneously and inseparably, and the second provides essential orientation and illumination to the first. Barth's description of this twofold dialogue is worth quoting (and elaborating upon) at length.

> What is involved is always the hearing of the Word of God, documented in the Bible, in any given present, since that necessarily precedes any speaking. Because the present is continually changing, the theologian cannot be content with establishing and communicating the results obtained by some classical period; his reflection must be renewed constantly. For this reason, serious theological work is forced, again and again, to begin from the beginning. However, as this is done, the theology of past periods, classical and less classical, also plays a part and demands a hearing. It demands a hearing as surely as it occupies

9. *ET*, 175.
10. *ET*, 174.

a place with us in the context of the Church. The
Church does not stand in a vacuum. Beginning from
the beginning, however necessary, cannot be a matter
of beginning off one's own bat. We have to remember
the communion of saints, bearing and being borne
by each other, asking and being asked, having to take
mutual responsibility for and among the sinners gath-
ered together in Christ. As regards theology, also,
we cannot be in the Church without taking as much
responsibility for the theology of the past, as for the
theology of our present. Augustine, Thomas Aquinas, Luther, Schleiermacher, and all the rest are not
dead but living. They still speak and demand a hearing as living voices, as surely as we know that they and
we belong together in the Church. They made in their
time the same contribution to the task of the Church
that is required of us today. As we make our contribution, they join in with theirs, and we cannot play our
part today without allowing them to play theirs. Our
responsibility is not only to God, to ourselves, to the
people of today, to other living theologians, but to
them. There is no past in the Church, so there is no
past in theology. "In him they all live."[11]

11. Karl Barth, *Protestant Theology in the Nineteenth Century: Its
Background and History*, trans. Brian Cozens and John Bowden (Grand
Rapids: Eerdmans, 2002), 3.

Theological paragraphs are rarely this instructive. While Barth does not draw out the pedagogical significance of these remarks, his reflections have a number of broad implications for the practice of teaching Christian theology. When we read just beneath the surface, a few basic principles emerge.

Good teachers remember that the secondary conversation is for the sake of the primary conversation. Since Christian theology is not a set of conceptual improvements upon Scripture, the purpose of teaching Christian theology is not to provide students with a system of thought that renders Scriptural interpretation unnecessary. Our aim is to lead students more deeply into the subject matter to which Scripture bears witness, and we cannot do that apart from the history of Christian reflection on Scripture. But knowledge of that history is valuable just to the extent that it helps students hear and respond to the Word of God that continually addresses them anew and afresh through the prophets and apostles.

Good teachers train students to read with sympathetic attention. Whether face-to-face or through the medium of literature, skillful conversation partners are secure enough to open themselves to one another, patient enough to listen carefully, and modest enough to assume they have something to learn. They do not hurry.[12] They calmly suspend judgment. They interpret claims fairly and in the best possible light, attempting to discern what the other is not only saying but also *trying* to say. If this sounds naive or idealistic, if one objects that this is not how most academic conversations work, that may have as much to do with the current climate of academic and theological culture as it does with any inherent weakness in this approach. The dominant ethos of scholarship within the humanities—and in much theological scholarship—is critique. The default option is to read with suspicion and skepticism, "to interrogate, unmask, expose, subvert, unravel, demystify, destabilize, take issue, and take umbrage."[13] Rather than representing one among many useful interpretive strategies, suspicious reading has become synonymous with serious scholarly investigation: "For many scholars in the humanities, it is not one good thing but the only imaginable thing."[14] Once habituated to critique, it becomes second nature

12. Many students are bothered by how slowly they read. Yet, to a person, the students I teach become better readers as they become slower readers.

13. Rita Felski, *The Limits of Critique* (Chicago: University of Chicago Press, 2015), 5.

14. Felski, *Limits of Critique*, 7.

to read with "guardedness rather than openness, aggression rather than submission, irony rather than reverence."[15] And yet, despite its hegemony, there are strong theological (and non-theological) reasons to be suspicious of ubiquitous suspicion—not least of which is that suspicious readers don't generate conversations as interesting and fruitful as do readers who befriend the texts they interpret.[16]

Good teachers do not train students to uncritically repeat the theology of the past. This claim does not contradict those I made in the previous paragraph. The appropriate response to the hypertrophy of critique is not to abandon criticism altogether. Criticism is essential to good conversation. Although an oppressive master, critical analysis is an indispensable servant. Every important text contains weaknesses, errors, lacunae, and prejudices, and good conversation partners do not allow such defects to go unnoticed or unchallenged. Nor do their colleagues want them to. Serious dialogue partners seek criticism. They invite

15. Felski, *Limits of Critique*, 21.

16. Felski makes the strongest case of which I am aware. Importantly, her aim is not to eliminate critique but "to de-essentialize the practice of suspicious reading by disinvesting it of presumptions of inherent rigor or intrinsic radicalism—thereby freeing up literary studies to embrace a wider range of affective styles and modes of argument" (*Limits of Critique*, 2).

disagreement. They hope others will understand them better than they understand themselves. We are not being responsible to the conversation of Christian theology when we freeze, repeat, and defend one of its classical periods, however illuminating that period happens to be. While we cannot do our work without our predecessors, our predecessors cannot do our work for us. We initiate students into the theology of yesterday because we believe that doing so helps them become better theologians *today*—not by imposing mandates for belief, or tracing lines outside of which students may not trespass, but by offering essential resources otherwise unavailable to them. Theological reasoning is always more timely, urgent, and creative when nourished by an abiding gratitude for the church's theological history and a willingness to be instructed by it. But the church is not "an institute of antiquities," and it does not read for primarily historical reasons.[17] While attentive to matters of historical context, we honor and acknowledge the authority of our forebears not when we train students to genuflect to them but when we help students enter into creative dialogue with them—dialogue that includes not

17. *CD* 1.2:619.

only careful and sympathetic attention but also the freedom to register disagreement, to develop familiar arguments in new directions, and to continually test everything against the witness of Scripture and the wisdom of the whole church. As Barth once noted, "It is not the point to become servants of some particular 'Fathers.' The only thing that matters is the one person: Christ."[18]

Good teachers train students to read widely. Traditions are always susceptible to a hardening of the arteries, to self-congratulatory insularity, to confusing their distinctive theological insights and emphases with the reality of the living God. To guard against these and similar tendencies, students need to step outside their familiar surroundings, read beyond the bounds of their particular ecclesial communities, and enter into dialogue with people who think very differently than they think. Doing so deepens knowledge and appreciation of one's own tradition and at the same time cultivates a healthy skepticism toward that tradition— skepticism that guards against parochial prejudice and self-righteous triumphalism. Alternatively, when

18. Karl Barth, *Barth in Conversation*, ed. Eberhard Busch, trans. The Translation Fellows of the Center for Barth Studies Princeton Theological Seminary, vol. 1, *1959–1962* (Louisville: Westminster John Knox, 2017), 26.

a spirit of insularity and zealous partisanship takes root in students, when they begin to envision themselves as warriors defending their ecclesial traditions and preferred theologians, they cut themselves off from the full wealth of the church's inheritance, which always makes them worse theologians. When gratitude for their communities devolves into hostility toward outsiders, when Christian students forget they are members of the one body of Christ, participants in the one communion of saints, they become grumpy theological gladiators rather than credible witnesses to Christ. And very often when this happens, students are simply mirroring similar patterns they see in their teachers.

Good teachers, however, consistently work against these attitudes by modeling expansive (and charitable) reading habits. They encourage students to explore unfamiliar territory and open themselves to new voices. They train students to savor the meat of a book rather than grind their teeth on its bones. They do not assume the air of prosecuting attorneys, nor do they train students to divide theologians into heroes and villains. In fact, they prefer not to discuss theologians they find repugnant and cannot make sing—people from whom they have learned nothing, about whom they have nothing good to say, and whose arguments they cannot describe generously and in their strongest possible forms. Very often, they teach in a mode of "inspired impersonation," whereby they assume an author's point of view and make it as vivid and compelling as possible to students.[19] Once again, none of this precludes criticism, disagreement, or even censure. But it does mean that denunciation never takes center stage in the classroom, and critique is always preceded by generous appreciation.[20] Barth sums up the spirit of this point when he writes,

> The theology of any period must be strong and free enough to give a calm, attentive and open hearing not only to the voices of the Church Fathers, not only to favorite voices, not only to the voices of the classical past, but to all the voices of the past. God is the Lord of the Church. He is also the Lord of theology. We cannot anticipate which of our fellow-workers from the past are welcome in our own work and which are not. It may always be that we have especial need of

19. Mark Edmundson, *Why Teach? In Defense of a Real Education* (New York: Bloomsbury, 2013), 201.

20. Barth's rule for criticizing Friedrich Schleiermacher applies to lesser figures as well: "Anyone who has never loved here . . . may not hate here either" (*Protestant Theology in the Nineteenth Century*, 413). Lamentably, the history of Christian theology is littered with influential figures who consistently transgressed this rule, and uncharitable theological scholarship remains a conspicuous problem today.

quite unsuspected (and among these, of quite unwelcome) voices in one sense or another.[21]

Good teachers train students to read with a willingness to be corrected. Responsible reading is a dialectical process of conversation between the reader and the text and presupposes a willingness to open oneself to critique. At some point it dawns on you that the very best books are reading you. They expose and illuminate you, cut through your ignorance and self-deception, challenge your misconceptions, and reveal you to yourself. We read because we are not yet who we want to be, because our knowledge and our lives are not yet what we think they could or should be. Otherwise, why bother? We truly enter into dialogue with a book only when we become willing to read "against ourselves."[22] Apart from a basic posture of openness, a readiness to be examined, corrected, and instructed, reading becomes an act of self-protection and thus a waste of time.

Good teachers do not speak the final word. Since our knowledge of God is limited, so too is our speech about

21. Barth, *Protestant Theology in the Nineteenth Century*, 3.

22. See Dietrich Bonhoeffer's comment, "We prefer our own thoughts to those of the Bible. We no longer read the Bible seriously. We read it no longer *against* ourselves but only *for* ourselves" (*DBWE* 11:377–78).

God. While God perfectly reveals himself in Christ, our reception of revelation is imperfect, and our doctrinal claims are always subject to correction and improvement. Thus teachers are not responsible for providing students with tidy conceptual schemes that eliminate theological loose ends and smooth out the ambiguities of experience. Our understanding does not seamlessly conform to God's reality, and instruction that suggests otherwise inevitably distorts the truth. The explanatory power such instruction generates is a mark of propaganda, not faithful Christian witness. Good teachers do not make Christianity easier for students by providing them with counterfeit clarity. If anything, they "jack up the price" by leading students more deeply into the subject matter, which in turn generates even more profound questions.[23] We make fools of ourselves and we fail our students when we teach as though our views (or those of our favorite theologians) are the definitive

23. Quoted in Sylvia Walsh, *Living Christianly: Kierkegaard's Dialectic of Christian Existence* (University Park: Pennsylvania State University Press, 2005), 6. On this point, see also Barth's comment, "While the congregation primarily brings to the church the great question of life and seeks an answer for it, on the contrary, the Bible primarily brings an answer, and it seeks the question to this answer. It seeks questioning people who want to seek and find this answer; who in so doing understand that its seeking of them is the very answer to their question" (*The Word of God and Theology*, trans. Amy Marga [London: T&T Clark, 2011], 117).

conclusion to a previously unsatisfactory history of reflection. To be clear, recognizing one's fallibility does not lead to equivocation, endless qualification, or theological indecision. In fact, quite the opposite. Epistemic humility is the condition for the possibility of truly free and confident theological speech.

> Being truly liberal means thinking and speaking in responsibility and openness on all sides, backwards and forwards, toward both past and future, and with what I might call a total personal modesty. To be modest is not to be skeptical; it is to see what one thinks and says also has limits. This does not hinder me from saying very definitely what I think I see and know. But I can do this only with the awareness that there have been and are other people before and alongside me, and that others still will come after me. This awareness gives me inner peace, so that I do not think I always have to be right even though I do say definitely what I say and think. Knowing that a limit is set for me too, I can move cheerfully within it as a free person.[24]

The frame of mind Barth describes here—at once humble and confident, modest and courageous, disciplined

24. Karl Barth, *Final Testimonies*, ed. Eberhard Busch, trans. Geoffrey Bromiley (Grand Rapids: Eerdmans, 1977), 34–35.

and free—befits teachers called to bear witness to a God they neither possess nor control. And when students encounter such teachers—deeply informed teachers who say what they think but do not always have to be right, teachers committed to the truth but aware of the limitations of their vision and thus receptive to criticism and correction—this often has a salutary effect on them. Exposure to this mind-set encourages students to loosen their grip on the fears and insecurities that keep them from exploring the subject matter more deeply, and that, in turn, increases their willingness to participate in classroom dialogue. I will say more about this in a moment, but first a general observation about classroom conversations.

Cultivating Classroom Conversations

If you know what's going to happen before you enter the classroom, you're doing it wrong. The best theological classrooms are full of conversation, and conversations cannot be choreographed—at least not real conversations between people hoping to seriously engage with one another, rather than merely deliver settled conclusions, speak on behalf of constituencies, or perform for an audience. In the back-and-forth of genuine dialogue, we cannot be certain of what students will say or even what we ourselves will say, and that instability is one of the reasons good conversations are so exhilarating and important. Conversations reveal commitments that require closer examination, beliefs that need to be sharpened or discarded, assumptions that cannot withstand sustained scrutiny. Pressed with challenging questions and confronted with troublesome counterevidence, we find ourselves recognizing new problems, making unexpected claims, revising long-standing beliefs, and discovering new lines of inquiry. Few things in academic life are as thrilling, humanizing, or instructive as illuminating conversations.

But the instability that makes good conversations stimulating also makes them risky. Conversations are improvisational, and improvisation is precarious. Unscripted dialogue does not afford us the luxury of extended reflection, and thinking on our feet can get us in trouble. In the heat of the moment, our reasoning goes wrong, we misunderstand one another, we reveal more than we intend, and we say things we don't mean or immediately regret. For these and other reasons, teachers and students often reach an unspoken agreement. Rather than entering into spirited back-and-forth dialogue, students allow teachers to deliver prepared remarks from behind their podiums, and teachers allow students to listen silently at their desks. The threat of real dialogue is exchanged for the safety of scripted monologue. And while this arrangement allows teachers to cover more material (and maintain more control), the losses significantly outweigh the gains, since students are afforded no opportunity to imaginatively explore and critically engage the material in real time. In such circumstances, students learn no more by coming to class than they would if they stayed at home and watched a recording or read a transcript of the lecture. To be clear, this is not a rejection of lectures per se, but rather a style of lecture that leaves no room for students to raise questions, express critical reservations, and otherwise engage in probing discussion of the material.

But suppose a teacher agrees that theological education flourishes in the soil of creative and rigorous conversation. How does one go about cultivating such conversation in the classroom, especially when students are, initially at least, less eager than ever to participate? The first and most obvious thing to say is that there is no universal template to follow, no ready-made formula to implement. Once again, teaching is an art, and art cannot be standardized. Learning to teach in one's own voice, to inhabit the classroom in one's own authentic way, is far more difficult than it sounds, which is one of the reasons I have thus far made no attempt to provide concrete guidance about how to implement the kind of teaching I describe in this book. But every semester I watch students shed their hesitation to engage in theological dialogue—students who, at the beginning of the semester, are unwilling to speak in public but by the end of the semester are participating eagerly in lively theological conversations. And as I've reflected on that experience, I've noticed a few things that other teachers may find useful as they develop their own approaches to classroom dialogue.

Students need room to fail. In addition to the ordinary fears and limitations that keep students from speaking in public, students studying theology are often gripped by an additional anxiety that stems from a tendency to conflate theological error with spiritual failure. For such students, each class session becomes a high-stakes examination of their nearness to God, an evaluation of their spiritual maturity. Possessed by this mind-set, students become cautious and guarded. They worry that admitting ignorance or unwittingly embracing falsehood may reveal their impiety, or perhaps even jeopardize their souls. Afraid of getting lost, they refuse to explore unfamiliar territory. Frightened of failure, they become unwilling to take risks. Needless to say, theological education does not flourish in these conditions. To fully engage with the material, students need freedom to raise fundamental questions, contemplate threatening ideas, challenge conventional wisdom, and draw fresh conclusions without fear of divine punishment or social disapproval. And that freedom is exactly what Jesus Christ provides. The eternal love of God enacted and revealed in Christ is the fresh air and solid ground of theological study. God's love is the unwavering reality that provides students the permission they need to ask theological questions without fear of penalty: "There is no fear in love, but perfect love casts out fear; for fear has to do with punishment, and whoever fears has not reached perfection in love" (1 John 4:18).

Students respond to penetrating questions. Throughout the Gospels, Jesus reveals himself through penetrating questions—questions that puncture cherished illusions and place his conversation partners in the position of having to decide how they will respond to him.[25]

25. See G. B. Caird's comment, "The whole tenor of the New Testament is opposed to dogmatism and authoritarianism. Jesus is represented

"What do you want?"

"Why are you afraid?"

"Who do you say that I am?"

"Do you love me?"

"Does this offend you?"

"What were you arguing about?"

"Are you asleep?"

Questions like these drive listeners to assess their basic commitments, examine the orientation of their lives, and decide where they stand in relationship to Jesus. They move theological reflection out of the realm of abstract speculation into the realm of existence. And while the specific questions Jesus asks emerge from his position of unique authority—an authority different in kind from that which every other teacher

in the Gospels as regularly teaching by questions and seeking to elicit a critical judgment from his hearers" (*New Testament Theology*, ed. L. D. Hurst [New York: Oxford University Press, 1994], 8).

possesses—his use of probing inquiry to personalize theological reflection is a model for all subsequent theological education. Once students become convinced that their teachers are for them and not against them, once they see their teachers assume a position of solidarity alongside them rather than superiority over them, they become receptive to questions that interrupt and examine habitual patterns of thinking and living. They invite such questions and grow to expect them. Few things are more stimulating to classroom conversation than questions that penetrate to the heart of students' deepest concerns.

Don't answer your own questions. Like good therapists, good teachers allow students to do their own work. When the wheels are turning, when students are absorbed in the questions, the sum of pedagogical wisdom is to step out of the way. Interrupting the process by supplying answers to questions that have not had time to ripen undermines emerging theological reason. Students need time to feel the weight of the questions, and for that to happen, teachers need to know when to stay silent. As the lights turn on, as students struggle with the subject matter, our assistance is needed "no more than a maiden needs a barber to shave her beard and no more than a bald man needs a hairdresser to 'style' his hair."[26] Extraordinary things happen in the classroom when teachers learn to wait five or ten seconds longer than feels comfortable before they start talking again. Indeed, few pedagogical practices are more important than the skillful use of awkward silence.[27]

Students hate when you don't understand their questions. It is impossible to facilitate good conversations if you are inattentive to what your students are saying—indeed, to what they are attempting to say. Few things are more discouraging to students than teachers who do not understand their questions. Even one or two uncomprehending responses will cause most students to

26. Søren Kierkegaard, *The Book on Adler*, ed. and trans. Howard V. Hong and Edna H. Hong (Princeton: Princeton University Press, 1998), 34.

27. See Dieter Rams's summarizing principle of good design: "Good design is as little design as possible" (*Weniger aber besser = Less but Better*, trans. Christopher Harrington [Berlin: Gestalten, 2016], 7). Good design is based on careful attention to how human beings inhabit and experience the world, and the questions designers ask, as well as the basic principles that inform their work, are an invaluable resource for designing and teaching theology courses. I doubt many theologians spend much time thinking about design, but good theology is often obscured by bad teaching, and bad teaching is often a symptom of bad design. If theology teachers were to become familiar with a simple book like William Lidwell's *Universal Principles of Design*—or, even better, if we were to start paying close attention to the way designers like Rams, Stefan Sagmeister, and Rachel Halvorson approach their work—our teaching would almost certainly improve.

go silent. When teachers fail to understand questions, students stop asking them, and when that happens, classroom conversation comes to an end. Teachers who do not listen to their students end up with students who do not listen to their teachers. As Dietrich Bonhoeffer observed, "We do God's work for our brothers and sisters when we learn to listen to them. . . . Those who cannot listen long and patiently will always be talking past others, and finally no longer will even notice it. Those who think their time is too precious to spend listening will never really have time for God and others, but only for themselves and for their own words and plans."[28]

However sentimental it sounds to say so, it is nevertheless true that our teaching is always worse when we assume we have nothing to learn from students. Apart from an abiding expectation that our students will become our teachers, our courses lack the urgency and electricity that characterize vital conversations. Students can tell when this expectation is missing, when their teachers don't expect them to say anything instructive or illuminating, and this awareness keeps our courses from coming fully to life. There may be

28. *DBWE* 5:98.

academic disciplines where this is not the case, or where teachers only infrequently learn from their students, but Christian theology is not one of them.

> To be a teacher is not to say: This is the way it is, nor is it to assign lessons and the like. No, to be a teacher is truly to be the learner. Instruction begins with this, that you, the teacher, learn from the learner, place yourself in what he has understood. . . . This is why I continually have inwardly raised an objection to a certain party of the orthodox here, that they band together in a little circle and strengthen one another in thinking that they are the only Christians— and thus do not know anything else to do with all Christendom than to declare that they are not Christians.[29]

Encourage charitable disagreement. Each class is a little community of people interacting with one another, and the social dynamics of the classroom are epistemologically significant. They condition the way students perceive the subject matter. Unfortunately, American universities (and churches) today, whether

29. Søren Kierkegaard, *The Point of View*, ed. and trans. Howard V. Hong and Edna H. Hong (Princeton: Princeton University Press, 1998), 46–47.

conservative or progressive, tend to socialize students into ideological conformity. They apply pressure on people to conform to prevailing opinion. This is altogether bad. Whereas education (including theological education) thrives in social contexts that encourage the robust exchange of a wide range of competing beliefs and commitments, it withers in contexts that do not. When intellectual diversity is frowned upon or prohibited, whether formally or informally, when teachers and students become unwilling or unable to graciously disagree with one another, genuine education suffers. The classrooms of teachers who dismiss serious but unpopular opinions eventually become places of deadening intellectual sameness, where opposing voices are silenced, underlying assumptions go unchallenged (and often unexpressed), social cohesion is consolidated through suspicion and denunciation of nonconforming outsiders, and transformative education is severely attenuated.

Excellent texts generate excellent conversations. A good teacher cannot overcome a bad syllabus, but a good syllabus covers a multitude of sins. If you assign strong readings, your courses have a chance of succeeding. If you assign weak readings, your courses will fail. The best classroom conversations are grounded in texts that everyone in the room has read carefully. The simplest way to motivate students to read carefully is to assign excellent texts and to give reading quizzes on those texts that count for a significant percentage of the overall course grade. When both of those conditions are met, most students will at least attempt to read with attention and care, and when that happens, classroom conversations are always more informed and illuminating. The best courses generate conversations that continue outside the classroom, filter back into the classroom, and continue once the semester ends. We must continually remind ourselves that we are training students to participate in the conversation of Christian theology until they die, not until the course ends. Like education generally, theological education is not something one acquires once and for all. The limits of our intelligence, experience, and wisdom, not to mention the subject matter of theology itself, preclude finality. In good theology courses, students will encounter at least one or two authors who become lifelong conversation partners. If that does not happen consistently in your courses—or if you notice that most students sell their books at the end of the semester—you may need to start assigning different books.

A Kierkegaardian Coda

Søren Kierkegaard despised the idea that theological reflection exists for its own sake. His belief that Christian existence is "essentially action" was a central theme of his authorship as a whole, and he repeatedly warned against the danger of allowing theological scholarship to obstruct and delay Christian discipleship.[30] We would do well to bear this warning in mind. Theological conversation is not an end in itself. Its purpose is to help students encounter the truth, discover their lives in Christ, and follow him into the world he loves. If the conversations that take place in our classes have the opposite effect on students, if students acquire the habit of talking about God objectively and dispassionately, if they come to believe that the truth can be known without being lived, learned without being appropriated, and if the accumulation of theological ideas results not in existential transformation and faithful witness but in endless talking and permanent postponement of decision and action, then our teaching works against the work of the Holy Spirit. As Kierkegaard himself expressed this conviction,

30. Søren Kierkegaard, *For Self-Examination and Judge for Yourself!*, ed. and trans. Howard V. Hong and Edna H. Hong (Princeton: Princeton University Press, 1990), 7.

"Wherever God is in truth, there he is always creating. He does not want a person to be spiritually soft and to bathe in the contemplation of his glory, but in becoming known by a person he wants to create in that person a new human being."[31] Kierkegaard devoted much of his career to advancing this basic thesis, and perhaps the most vivid and compelling expression of this conviction is found in a famous journal entry, which he wrote, not coincidentally, while studying for a degree in theology. His description of the relationship between the truth of the gospel and his own lived existence is a fitting conclusion to this chapter, and indeed to this book as a whole.

> What I really need is to be clear about *what I am to do*, not what I must know, except in the way knowledge must precede all action. It is a question of understanding my own destiny, of seeing what the Deity really wants *me* to do; the thing is to find a truth which is truth *for me*, to find *the idea for which I am willing to live and die.* . . . What use would it be to be able to propound the meaning of Christianity, to explain many separate facts, if it had no deeper meaning for

31. Søren Kierkegaard, *Eighteen Upbuilding Discourses*, ed. and trans. Howard V. Hong and Edna H. Hong (Princeton: Princeton University Press, 1990), 325.

myself and *my life*? . . . What use would it be if truth were to stand there before me, cold and naked, not caring whether I acknowledge it or not, inducing an anxious shiver rather than trusting devotion? Certainly I won't deny that I still accept an *imperative of knowledge*, and that through it one can also influence people, but *then it must be taken up alive in me*, and *this* is what I now see as the main point. It is this my soul thirsts for as the African deserts thirst for water.[32]

32. *KJN*, 1:19–20.

BIBLIOGRAPHY

Alter, Adam. *Irresistible: The Rise of Addictive Technology and the Business of Keeping Us Hooked.* New York: Penguin, 2017.

Augustine. *Teaching Christianity.* Translated by Edmund Hill. Vol. 11 of *The Works of Saint Augustine: A Translation for the 21st Century*, edited by John E. Rotelle. Hyde Park, NY: New City Press, 1990–2005.

Barth, Karl. *Barth in Conversation.* Vol. 1, *1959–1962.* Edited by Eberhard Busch. Translated by The Translation Fellows of the Center for Barth Studies Princeton Theological Seminary. Louisville: Westminster John Knox, 2017.

———. *Church Dogmatics.* Vol. 1.1, *The Doctrine of the Word of God.* 2nd ed. Edited by G. W. Bromiley and T. F. Torrance. Translated by G. W. Bromiley. Edinburgh: T&T Clark, 1975.

———. *Church Dogmatics.* Vol. 1.2, *The Doctrine of the Word of God.* Edited by G. W. Bromiley and T. F. Torrance. Translated by G. T. Thomson and Harold Knight. Edinburgh: T&T Clark, 1956.

———. *Church Dogmatics.* Vol. 2.1, *The Doctrine of God.* Edited by G. W. Bromiley and T. F. Torrance. Translated by T. H. L. Parker et al. Edinburgh: T&T Clark, 1957.

———. *Church Dogmatics.* Vol. 2.2, *The Doctrine of God.* Edited by G. W. Bromiley and T. F. Torrance. Translated by G. W. Bromiley, J. C. Campbell et al. Edinburgh: T&T Clark, 1957.

————. *Church Dogmatics*. Vol. 3.2, *The Doctrine of Creation*. Edited by G. W. Bromiley and T. F. Torrance. Translated by G. W. Bromiley et al. Edinburgh: T&T Clark, 1960.

————. *Church Dogmatics*. Vol. 4.1, *The Doctrine of Reconciliation*. Edited by G. W. Bromiley and T. F. Torrance. Translated by G. W. Bromiley. Edinburgh: T&T Clark, 1956.

————. *Church Dogmatics*. Vol. 4.2, *The Doctrine of Reconciliation*. Edited by G. W. Bromiley and T. F. Torrance. Translated by G. W. Bromiley. Edinburgh: T&T Clark, 1958.

————. *Church Dogmatics*. Vol. 4.3.1, *The Doctrine of Reconciliation*. Edited by G. W. Bromiley and T. F. Torrance. Translated by G. W. Bromiley. Edinburgh: T&T Clark, 1961.

————. *Church Dogmatics*. Vol. 4.3.2, *The Doctrine of Reconciliation*. Edited by G. W. Bromiley and T. F. Torrance. Translated by G. W. Bromiley. Edinburgh: T&T Clark, 1962.

————. *The Epistle to the Romans*. Translated by Edwyn C. Hoskyns. Oxford: Oxford University Press, 1968.

————. *Evangelical Theology: An Introduction*. Translated by Grover Foley. Grand Rapids: Eerdmans, 1963.

————. *Final Testimonies*. Edited by Eberhard Busch. Translated by Geoffrey Bromiley. Grand Rapids: Eerdmans, 1977.

————. *Protestant Theology in the Nineteenth Century: Its Background and History*. Translated by Brian Cozens and John Bowden. Grand Rapids: Eerdmans, 2002.

————. *The Word of God and Theology*. Translated by Amy Marga. London: T&T Clark, 2011.

Barth, Karl, and Eduard Thurneysen. "Jesus and Nicodemus." In *Come Holy Spirit: Sermons*, translated by George W. Richards, Elmer G. Homrighausen, and Karl J. Ernst, 101–11. New York: Round Table Press, 1933.

Bonhoeffer, Dietrich. *Dietrich Bonhoeffer Works*. Vol. 4, *Disciple-ship*. Edited by Geffrey B. Kelly and John D. Godsey. Trans-lated by Barbara Green and Reinhard Krauss. Minneapolis: Fortress, 2003.

———. *Dietrich Bonhoeffer Works*. Vol. 5, *Life Together and Prayerbook of the Bible*. Edited by Geffrey B. Kelly. Translated by Daniel W. Bloesch and James H. Burtness. Minneapolis: Fortress, 1996.

———. *Dietrich Bonhoeffer Works*. Vol. 6, *Ethics*. Edited by Clifford J. Green. Translated by Reinhard Krauss et al. Min-neapolis: Fortress, 2009.

———. *Dietrich Bonhoeffer Works*. Vol. 8, *Letters and Papers from Prison*. Edited by John W. de Gruchy. Translated by Isabel Best et al. Minneapolis: Fortress, 2009.

———. *Dietrich Bonhoeffer Works*. Vol. 11, *Ecumenical, Aca-demic, and Pastoral Work: 1931–1932*. Edited by Victoria J. Barnett et al. Translated by Douglas W. Stott et al. Minne-apolis: Fortress, 2012.

———. *Dietrich Bonhoeffer Works*. Vol. 13, *London: 1933–1935*. Edited by Keith W. Clements. Translated by Isabel Best. Min-neapolis: Fortress, 2007.

———. *Dietrich Bonhoeffer Works*. Vol. 14, *London: 1933–1935*. Edited by Mark Brocker and H. Gaylon Barker. Translated by Douglas W. Stott. Minneapolis: Fortress, 2013.

Busch, Eberhard. *The Great Passion: An Introduction to Karl Barth's Theology*. Edited by Darrell L. Guder and Judith Guder. Translated by Geoffrey W. Bromiley. Grand Rapids: Eerdmans, 2004.

Caird, G. B. *New Testament Theology*. Edited by L. D. Hurst. New York: Oxford University Press, 1994.

Casalis, George. *Portrait of Karl Barth*. Garden City, NY: Doubleday, 1963.

Edmundson, Mark. *Why Teach? In Defense of a Real Education*. New York: Bloomsbury, 2013.

Felski, Rita. *The Limits of Critique*. Chicago: University of Chicago Press, 2015.

González, Justo L. *The History of Theological Education*. Nashville: Abingdon, 2015.

Howard, Thomas Albert. *Protestant Theology and the Making of the Modern German University*. Oxford: Oxford University Press, 2006.

Jenson, Robert. *A Theology in Outline: Can These Bones Live?* New York: Oxford University Press, 2016.

Jowett, J. H. *The Preacher: His Life and Work*. New York: Hodder & Stoughton, 1912.

Kierkegaard, Søren. *The Book on Adler*. Edited and translated by Howard V. Hong and Edna H. Hong. Princeton: Princeton University Press, 1998.

———. *Concluding Unscientific Postscript to* Philosophical Fragments. Edited and translated by Howard V. Hong and Edna H. Hong. Princeton: Princeton University Press, 1992.

———. *Eighteen Upbuilding Discourses*. Edited and translated by Howard V. Hong and Edna H. Hong. Princeton: Princeton University Press, 1990.

———. *For Self-Examination and Judge for Yourself!* Edited and translated by Howard V. Hong and Edna H. Hong. Princeton: Princeton University Press, 1990.

———. *Kierkegaard's Journals and Notebooks*. Edited by Niels Jørgen Cappelørn et al. Vol. 1, *Journals AA–DD*. Princeton: Princeton University Press, 2007.

————. *Kierkegaard's Journals and Notebooks*. Edited by Niels Jørgen Cappelørn et al. Vol. 2, *Journals EE–KK*. Princeton: Princeton University Press, 2008.

————. *Kierkegaard's Journals and Notebooks*. Edited by Niels Jørgen Cappelørn et al. Vol. 4, *Journals NB–NB5*. Princeton: Princeton University Press, 2011.

————. *Kierkegaard's Journals and Notebooks*. Edited by Niels Jørgen Cappelørn et al. Vol. 5, *Journals NB6–10*. Princeton: Princeton University Press, 2011.

————. *Kierkegaard's Journals and Notebooks*. Edited by Niels Jørgen Cappelørn et al. Vol. 6, *Journals NB11–14*. Princeton: Princeton University Press, 2012.

————. *Kierkegaard's Journals and Notebooks*. Edited by Niels Jørgen Cappelørn et al. Vol. 8, *Journals NB21–25*. Princeton: Princeton University Press, 2015.

————. *Kierkegaard's Journals and Notebooks*. Edited by Niels Jørgen Cappelørn et al. Vol. 9, *Journals NB26–NB30*. Princeton: Princeton University Press, 2017.

————. *Kierkegaard's Journals and Notebooks*. Edited by Niels Jørgen Cappelørn et al. Vol. 10, *Journals NB31–36*. Princeton: Princeton University Press, 2018.

————. *The Moment and Late Writings*. Edited and translated by Howard V. Hong and Edna H. Hong. Princeton: Princeton University Press, 1998.

————. *Philosophical Fragments*. Edited and translated by Howard V. Hong and Edna H. Hong. Princeton: Princeton University Press, 1985.

————. *The Point of View*. Edited and translated by Howard V. Hong and Edna H. Hong. Princeton: Princeton University Press, 1998.

————. *Practice in Christianity*. Edited and translated by Howard V. Hong and Edna H. Hong. Princeton: Princeton University Press, 1991.

————. *The Sickness unto Death*. Edited and translated by Howard V. Hong and Edna H. Hong. Princeton: Princeton University Press, 1980.

————. *Three Discourses on Imagined Occasions*. Edited and translated by Howard V. Hong and Edna H. Hong. Princeton: Princeton University Press, 1993.

Lewis, C. S. *God in the Dock: Essays on Theology and Ethics*. Edited by Walter Hooper. Grand Rapids: Eerdmans, 1970.

Neder, Adam. *Participation in Christ: An Entry into Karl Barth's "Church Dogmatics."* Louisville: Westminster John Knox, 2009.

————. "'The Sun Behind the Clouds': Some Barthian Thoughts about Teaching Christian Theology." In *Karl Barth and the Making of "Evangelical Theology": A Fifty-Year Perspective*, edited by Clifford B. Anderson and Bruce L. McCormack, 222–35. Grand Rapids: Eerdmans, 2015.

Ponticus, Evagrius. *The Praktikos and Chapters on Prayer*. Translated by John Eudes Bamberger. Kalamazoo, MI: Cistercian Publications, 1972.

Purvis, Zachary. *Theology and the University in Nineteenth-Century Germany*. Oxford Theology and Religion Monographs. Oxford: Oxford University Press, 2016.

Rams, Dieter Rams. *Weniger, aber besser = Less, but Better*. Translated by Christopher Harrington. Berlin: Gestalten, 2016.

Rowe, C. Kavin. *One True Life: The Stoics and Early Christians as Rival Traditions*. New Haven: Yale University Press, 2016.

Smith, James K. A. *Desiring the Kingdom: Worship, Worldview, and Cultural Formation*. Grand Rapids: Baker Academic, 2009.

———. *You Are What You Love: The Spiritual Power of Habit.* Grand Rapids: Brazos, 2016.

Tietz, Christiane. "Karl Barth and Charlotte von Kirschbaum." *Theology Today* 74, no. 2 (July 2017): 86–111.

Turkle, Sherry. *Reclaiming Conversation: The Power of Talk in a Digital Age.* New York: Penguin, 2015.

Walsh, Sylvia. *Living Christianly: Kierkegaard's Dialectic of Christian Existence.* University Park: Pennsylvania State University Press, 2005.

Wood, Ralph C. *Flannery O'Connor and the Christ-Haunted South.* Grand Rapids: Eerdmans, 2004.

INDEX

acedia, 33, 76

anthropology, 5–7, 15–32. *See also* identity; image of God; Jesus Christ

Arcade Fire, 70

assessment, 35–36, 38, 88–90

attention, 116, 121–23

Augustine, 12, 35n30

authority, 3, 46–48, 74, 79–81, 104–5, 107–10, 123–25, 128–30

Barth, Karl
  on existence and truth, 74–75, 103
  on Feuerbach, Ludwig, 56–58
  on the Holy Spirit, 34–35
  on humility, 80–81
  influence on this book, 1, 7, 61–63
  on Jesus Christ and anthropology, 16–17
  on Jesus Christ and knowledge of God, 56–59
  on knowledge and existence, 40–41
  liberal, on being truly, 130
  on Nicodemus, 92–96
  on personal response to God, 87
  on reading Scripture, 118–20, 124–25
  on reconciliation, 19–20
  on revelation as reawakening, 109–10
  on risk in theology, 53
  on sin, 31
  on theology as conversation, 118–20
  on the vices of theologians, 62–69

Bible. *See* Holy Scripture
Bonhoeffer, Dietrich
    on acting without certainty,
        107
    on educational ideals, 36
    on following Jesus, 97–98
    influence on this book, 7
    on Jesus Christ and educa-
        tion, 25
    on knowledge and existence,
        41n5
    on listening, 139
    on reading Scripture, 128n22
    on sin, 31

certainty, 104–5, 107–10
choice. *See* decision
church, 9–10, 119–20, 124–26
classroom, as (un)safe space,
    85–112
conversation, 7, 93–96, 113–45
course evaluations, 88–90. *See
    also* assessment
credibility. *See* ethos
critique, 121–25

decision, 86–88, 92, 105–7
design, 138n27
disagreement, 122–25, 140–41

diversity, intellectual, 78–79,
    123–28, 140–41. *See also*
    disagreement

empathy, 116
ethos, 61–84, 100–103
existence
    as goal of education, 4,
        143–45
    and Jesus Christ, 10, 25–30
    and knowledge, 38–45
    and sin, 30–31
    of students, 105–10
    of teachers, 61–84
    theology's implications for,
        49–51, 91–92
    and witness, 71–77, 81–84,
        100–103
    See also decision; ethos

failure, 134–35
faith, 26–27, 39
Felski, Rita, 122–23
Feuerbach, Ludwig, 57

grace, 30, 35, 56, 92

habit, 6
Holy Scripture, 118–21

Holy Spirit, 6, 26, 32–35, 63–64

human nature. *See* anthropology

humility, 78–81, 130

identity, 6, 15–32. *See also* anthropology; existence; Jesus Christ

image of God, 18, 26

imagination, 44–45, 49–51, 90–92

indoctrination, 52–53, 78, 128–30, 140–41

Iniesta, Andrés, 81–84, 91–92

Jesus Christ
  conversations with, 93–96
  and education, 3, 135
  and existence, 25–29
  following, 96–99
  and identity, 6, 16–17
  knowledge of, 92–99
  and knowledge of God, 54–59
  and Nicodemus, 93–96
  as prophet, 34, 72
  and reconciliation, 18–24, 92
  seeks followers not admirers, 41–44
  against teachers, 70

teachers profit off, 76–77

teaching through questions, 135–37

Kierkegaard, Søren
  Christian, on becoming 38
  on contemporaneity, 4
  on decision, 106–9
  existence-communication, Christianity as 102–3
  on Feuerbach, Ludwig, 56
  influence on this book, 7
  against professors 41–44
  on sin, 31
  on teachers as learners, 140
  on truth and existence, 41–44, 69n13, 73–74, 109, 143–45
  on truth and God, 32n24

knowledge, 4–5, 37–59, 78–79, 107–10, 128–30

Lewis, C. S., 12

love, 64, 72, 96–98, 127n20, 135

McCormack, Bruce, 13

McLelland, Reginald, 11–13

mystery, divine, 54–56

Nicodemus, 92–96

peace, 24–25
prayer, 34–36
presence of God, 75–76, 100–101
projection, 56–59
pronouns for God, 5n5
propaganda. *See* indoctrination

questions, 135–40

Radiohead, 66
Rams, Dieter, 138n27
reading, 118–31, 141–42
reconciliation, 18–26, 92
reputation. *See* ethos; vanity
revelation, 3, 17, 32–34, 55, 59,
    109–10, 129
risk, 104–12, 132–33

self-examination, 77–78
silence, awkward, 138
sin, 30–32, 69
Smith, James K. A., 5–7
social conformity, 26–27, 140–41
socialization, 5, 28
social media, 115–18

theology, history of, 45–49
tradition, 123–28
truth
    and existence, 4, 40, 68–70,
        72–77, 92, 100–101, 108–9,
        143–45
    Jesus Christ as, 4, 41, 57–59
    perception of, 32n24, 78, 129
    as subjective, not subjectivist,
        44n12, 69, 78
    as unpossessable, 24–26, 32
Turkle, Sherry, 115–18

universities, 9–10, 140–41

vanity, 65–71
virtue, 5, 28

witness, 44n12, 71–77, 81–84,
    100–103

Yorke, Thom, 56